*exciting low carb recipes

essentials

carolyn humphries

foulsham
LONDON • NEW YORK • TORONTO • SYDNEY

foulsham

The Publishing House, Bennetts Close,
Cippenham, Slough, Berks, SL1 5AP, England

ISBN 0-572-03039-8

A CIP record for this book is available from the British Library

Printed in Great Britain by Cox & Wyman Ltd, Reading

Contents

Introduction

For most people the concept of a high-protein, low-carbohydrate diet seems fantastic. Platefuls of eggs and bacon for breakfast; an enormous chunk of cheese, maybe with a token tomato, for lunch; a huge slab of steak or even a whole chicken for dinner, and lashings of whipped cream on a bowl of jelly (jello) for pudding. Terrific, at least initially; but after a very short while the regime changes from satisfying and filling to just plain gross. When meals are unimaginative and very limited, the desire to carry on with the diet wanes. You find you actually miss fruit and vegetables – even if you thought you weren't that keen on them anyway – and you get sick of cream and butter. This is not how a low-carbohydrate diet should be.

The other problem is that most people don't read their diet book properly before they start. They don't really understand their bodies and what they need to eat to stay healthy. So they assume you just keep on eating huge amounts of protein, very few fruits and vegetables and absolutely no bread, pasta, rice or potatoes. This is not right either.

This book is designed to give you fantastic, imaginative, low-carbohydrate meals from morning to night. They are all carefully balanced to include low-carb serving suggestions so you get all the essential nutrients you need week in, week out.

You should enjoy every meal and eat enough to be comfortably full but you shouldn't gorge until you're fit to burst!

Take the time to read the simple information at the beginning of the book, which will help you understand the way a low-carbohydrate diet works. You will discover how to gradually build up your carbohydrates after the initial two-week, very-low-intake phase and then how to maintain a trim figure for life, eating fabulously into the bargain! Most of the recipes serve four but it is easy to quarter them if you are going to dine alone. By the way, the recipes are so tempting that even people not on a low-carb regime will love them too. (They can always 'top up' their portions with a little starchy carb – like toast for breakfast or a few potatoes for dinner – but advise them not to go overboard on their proteins as well or they'll be the ones needing to lose weight.) It's a good idea to purchase a carbohydrate counter (like my *The Hugely Better Carbohydrate Counter,* Foulsham, 0-572-02958-6) so you can check out everything you eat in the future.

How a Low-carbohydrate Diet Works

A low-carbohydrate diet is a very effective way to achieve weight loss. It is based on a few simple principles.

Carbohydrates are the starches and sugars contained in foods such as breads, cakes, rice, pasta and cereals, and also in fruit and vegetables. When we eat carbohydrates our body breaks them down into glucose to use as energy. If we eat more carbohydrates than our body burns, they are stored in the body as fat. But if we eat less than our body requires, the body is forced to burn body fat instead for energy, which results in weight loss.

To help the body absorb the glucose from the carbohydrates and turn it into energy, the pancreas produces insulin. The more starch and sugar we eat, the more insulin is produced. Insulin also helps the body to store any unused glucose as fat. If we severely restrict our intake of carbohydrates, the body reduces its production of insulin and so does not store body fat.

Reducing our intake of carbohydrates is a very efficient way of losing weight. In addition, once the body is free from large quantities of carbohydrates, blood sugar levels remain constant and our craving for sugary snacks is reduced, as well as any serious hunger pangs – clearly a useful aid for dieters.

It is not sensible to cut out carbohydrates entirely, however. Our bodies do need a small amount of glucose for some vital functions. This may be provided by the intake of a small quantity of carbohydrate or, alternatively if necessary, protein, which can be processed by the liver and turned into sugar.

Ketosis

One of the less attractive side effects of a low-carbohydrate diet is ketosis. This occurs when the liver begins to produce chemicals called ketones, from fatty acids, for energy. Any unused ketones cannot be turned back into fat and stored, so are excreted from the body in the urine. Ketosis causes severe bad breath and a metallic taste in the mouth. Some diets encourage such symptoms since they indicate that your body is burning fat but I prefer that ketosis should be avoided. If you start to experience these unpleasant symptoms when your carbohydrate intake is very low, eat a small raw carrot or half a red pepper. This will add 4–5 g of carb to your diet. You will still lose weight, although perhaps a little less rapidly. You can do this every time you suffer the symptoms.

Note: Ketosis is not the same thing as ketoacidosis, a dangerous condition that is suffered by diabetics when the blood sugar becomes acutely acidic and blood sugar levels soar. This may occur either because the body is not producing insulin or because it is not using it correctly, so it is not processing sugar for energy. The body then produces ketones for fuel instead.

The four-phase plan and how it works

Most low-carbohydrate plans are divided into four stages, or phases.

- The first is very low in carbohydrates to initiate a quick weight loss.
- The second and third phases are designed to help you lose weight while still eating a diet that contains all the nutrition your body needs.
- The last stage is a maintenance plan for when you've reached your goal and want to remain on a healthy eating regime for life.

Phase 1: Quick Weight Loss

Phase 1 is designed to kick-start your diet with an immediate rapid loss of weight. This is done by limiting your carbohydrate intake to just 20 g per day. But don't be tempted to have less than 20 g.

You can eat what you like, using any of the 'allowed' foods listed on pages 10–13, providing your daily intake does not exceed 20 g of carbohydrate. Try to eat five portions of fruit and vegetables a day from the permitted list, even from day one. It goes without saying you can substitute any meat, fish or poultry for another – you can eat as much of them as you like.

This regime should be followed for two weeks only. Do not be tempted to continue any longer, as the lack of carbohydrates can damage your health.

Top tip
Make a list of the meals you have over the next two weeks then you'll find it easy in week 3 (the first week of Phase 2 of the plan) to increase your carbohydrates as suggested. Recipes suitable for Phase 1 are marked with a ❶ but make sure they don't add up to more than 20 g of carbohydrate in a day.

Foods you are allowed

You must not exceed your daily allowance of 20 g of carbohydrates. The following list tells you which foods you can – or can't – eat.

Eat in unlimited quantities

Some foods do not contain any carbohydrates, so you can eat as much as you like. Where these are included in my recipes, you can have larger or smaller portions, depending on your appetite.

Pure meat and poultry

Pure fish and shellfish

All hard and fresh cheeses
Whey cheeses, such as ricotta, should be avoided during the first two weeks.

Olive, seed and vegetable oils

Butter, fresh creams and crème fraîche
Note that single (light) and soured (dairy sour) cream have 1 g carbohydrate per 15 ml/1 tbsp.

Eggs
These may be cooked in any way.

Sugar-free jelly (jello)

Eat in restricted quantities

Some foods you can eat only in specified quantities that keep within the carbohydrate allowance.

Vegetables

The carbohydrate counts below are based on an average-sized portion of 100 g/4 oz/3 heaped tbsp unless otherwise stated. You can eat only those vegetables that have a very low carbohydrate content, i.e. less than 10 g per portion.

Some low-carbohydrate diets say you shouldn't have carrots at this stage because they contain sugars. But when cooked they contain only 5 g carbohydrate (8 g in a large raw one) and are a good source of fibre, so I have included them.

Item	*Carb content per portion*
Artichoke hearts – 1 heart	1 g
Asparagus	2 g
Aubergine (eggplant) – ½ medium	3 g
Bamboo shoots	trace
Beansprouts – a good handful	1 g
Broccoli	2 g
Brussels sprouts	3 g
Cabbage, all types	2 g
Carrots	5 g
Cauliflower	2 g

Celeriac (celery root)	2 g
Courgettes (zucchini)	3 g
French (green) beans	5 g
Kale	1 g
Kohlrabi	5 g
Leeks	3 g
Mangetout (snow peas)	2 g
Marrow (squash)	2 g
Mushrooms, all types	trace
Okra (ladies' fingers)	3 g
Onions – 1 medium	7 g
Pak choi	2 g
Palm hearts – 1 piece	2 g
Pumpkin	2 g
Rhubarb	1 g
Runner beans	2 g
Spinach	1 g
Spring (collard) greens	2 g
Swede (rutabaga)	2 g
Swiss chard	4 g
Turnip	2 g
Water chestnuts	3 g

Fruit
Only a few fruits are permitted at this stage.

Item	Carb content per item
Avocado – 1 medium	3 g
Olives	trace
Tomato – 1 medium	2 g

Salad stuffs

Celery	1 g
Chicory (Belgian endive) – 1 medium	2 g
Cucumber – 5 slices	1 g
Fennel – ½ head	2 g
Fresh herbs	trace
Lettuce, all types – a good handful	1 g
(Bell) peppers – 1 medium	green 4 g
	yellow/orange 7 g
	red 10 g
Radishes	trace
Rocket – a good handful	trace
Sorrel – a good handful	trace
Watercress – a good handful	trace

Spices
You can eat all types provided there is no starchy filler or sugar.

Forbidden foods

You may not eat any of the following:

- Processed meat, poultry and fish products that contain carbohydrates, e.g. sausages, fish fingers, southern fried chicken – check the labels.
- Milk and yoghurt.
- Fruits, apart from the three listed on page 13.
- Starchy foods, such as bread, potatoes, pasta, rice or other grains.
- Sugar of any kind and foods containing any type of sugar. If you do need to sweeten anything, use a no-calorie artificial sweetener.

Drinks

More detailed drinks information is on pages 37–8 but as a guide at this stage:

- Drink plenty of water, including still, sparkling or no-calorie flavoured.
- You may drink pure lemon or lime juice, diluted with water, but no sweeter pure juices or any drinks sweetened with sugar.
- You may drink clear savoury drinks, like Bovril or those made from bouillon powder (but check the labels for carbohydrates).
- Ideally you should avoid alcohol for the first two weeks for maximum weight loss. If you don't want to give it up, you may have dry red or white wine and spirits (but only with

no-carbohydrate/diet mixers) as they contain at most just a trace of carbohydrate. Do not drink other alcoholic drinks like beer, cider or fortified and sweet wines as they contain carbohydrates (see the specific notes on page 38).

- Avoid caffeine or keep your intake low. Either have weak coffee or tea, or choose decaffeinated ones. Do not add milk; drink it black or with just a dash of cream. Coffee contains some carbohydrates so don't drink it in excess.

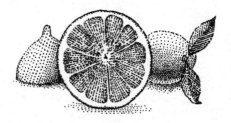

Phase 2:
Gradual Weight Loss

After two weeks, you progress to the second phase and start increasing your daily carbohydrate intake by a small amount each week until you find your optimum carb level and have almost reached your target weight.

For the first week you simply increase your daily intake of carbohydrates by 5 g. The easiest way is to include portions of the nuts and seeds listed on pages 19–20 to meals you've had for the first two weeks. For the next week add a further 10 g per day (making 35 g in total). From then on, each week increase your daily carbohydrates by 10 g (so 45 g the third week and so on).

You should continue to lose weight gradually, while including more carbohydrate in your diet, but if you find you start to put on weight again, cut back by 5 g or 10 g per day. It is rather like balancing a delicate set of scales: each person must find the level that suits them. We each burn carbs at a different rate, and this will also vary according to how active we are, so there are no hard-and-fast rules. Your weight loss must be gradual if it is to stay off in the long term. Trying to rush it by 'starving' yourself of carbohydrates won't work and you could harm your health.

During this phase, the range of foods you can eat is vastly increased (see pages 19–24). You can make up your meals, choosing ingredients from the lists of individual foods and any of the recipes I suggest, as long as every week you set your new carbohydrate intake and stick to it. For each food, I have given the carb content per portion so you can calculate your intake exactly. Weigh yourself each week during this phase. You should aim to increase your carbohydrates gradually, whilst still steadily continuing to lose weight, until you have nearly reached your target weight. Exactly how long this takes will depend on how much weight you have to lose and how fast your body burns fat.

The plateau

At some point during this phase or the next, you will probably hit an impasse when, for no apparent reason, the weight loss stops. Providing you are not actually gaining weight, your carbohydrate levels are about right. However, if your weight is going up again, you need to cut back on the carbohydrates. If the plateau happens during the next phase when you've started having 'treats' then, obviously, these should stop until you're losing weight again. Don't cut out the essential low-carbohydrate fruit and vegetables.

If, however, you still have a little bit to lose and it won't budge, try one of the following ways to re-start your weight loss.

- Eat only fruit for just one or two days, preferably when you don't have to work or be too energetic. Then continue as before.
- Cut down your carbs slightly by skipping your dessert for a day or two.
- Check whether you are consuming hidden carbohydrates (see pages 30–32) and, if you are, cut them out so you get back to the carbohydrate level you really want.
- Go on a calorie-controlled phase for a week or two, then go back to the low-carbohydrate regime and continue from there as before. Stick to 1,000–1,200 calories per day for a woman or 1,200–1,500 for a man (*The Hugely Better Carbohydrate Counter* will also give you the calorie content of everything you want to eat).

Don't be tempted to reduce the amount of allowed fruit and vegetables, protein and fats you are eating while staying on the low-carbohydrate diet. Contrary to what you might imagine, this will slow your metabolism right down so you won't lose weight at all – and you won't be getting the nutrients you need either.

Extra carb options for Phase 2

Remember, in the first week you'll simply be adding 5 g carb a day to the diet you've been eating for the last two weeks, then gradually increasing your carb count each week. To maintain a healthy variety – especially when you are adding perhaps 10 g or 15 g to your daily intake – you can, of course, split the portions between different foods.

Note: For precision, if you would rather weigh your foods:

- 1 tbsp = 7.5 g/¼ oz
- 3 heaped tbsp = 100 g/4 oz
- 4 tbsp = 25 g/1 oz/¼ cup

Nuts and seeds

These nuts and seeds are very low in carbohydrates but high in fibre.

Item	Quantity	Carb content
Almonds	4 tbsp	2 g
Brazils	4 tbsp	1 g
Cashews	4 tbsp	4 g
Coconut, desiccated	1 tbsp	1 g
Fennel seeds	1 tbsp	trace
Hazelnuts (filberts)	4 tbsp	1 g
Macadamias	4 tbsp	2 g
Mixed nuts	4 tbsp	2 g
Peanuts	4 tbsp	3 g
Pecans	4 tbsp	2 g
Pine nuts	4 tbsp	1 g
Pistachios	4 tbsp	2 g
Pumpkin seeds	1 tbsp	1 g

19

Sesame seeds	1 tbsp	trace
Sunflower seeds	1 tbsp	1 g
Walnuts	4 tbsp	1 g

If you want to eat all of one type of nut, you may not fancy munching your way through a large number, so a good way of enjoying them is to make a nut butter or cream.

For nut butter, purée the nuts in a blender or food processor, adding a dash of sunflower or nut oil to form a paste, stopping and scraping down the sides as necessary. Season with a tiny pinch of salt, if you like, then spread it in celery or chicory for a delicious snack.

For nut cream, purée the nuts in a blender or food processor with a little water (about 60 ml/4 tbsp per 50 g/ 2 oz/½ cup nuts) to form a soft dropping consistency. Sweeten with a little artificial sweetener. Chill until ready to serve on any of the desserts in the diet plan or with sugar-free jelly (jello) for a snack.

Fruits
With a higher carb intake, there's plenty to choose from.

Item	Quantity	Carb content
Apple	1 medium	15 g
Apricot, dried	1	3 g

Apricot, fresh	1	4 g
Banana slices, dried	small handful	10 g
Blackberries	3 heaped tbsp	5 g
Blackcurrants	3 heaped tbsp	7 g
Cherries	12	5 g
Clementine	1	6 g
Damson	1	1 g
Date, dried	1	10 g
Date, fresh	1	8 g
Fig, fresh	1	5 g
Gooseberries	3 heaped tbsp	2 g
Grapefruit	½	6 g
Grapes	100 g/4 oz	15 g
Greengage	1	2 g
Guava	1	5 g
Kiwi fruit	1 small	10 g
Kumquat	1	3 g
Lychee	1	1 g
Mandarin orange	1	7 g
Mango	½ medium	15 g
Melon	1 large wedge	15 g
Nectarine	1 medium	15 g
Orange	1 medium	15 g
Papaya (pawpaw)	½ medium	15 g
Passion fruit	1	4 g
Peach	1 medium	15 g

Pear . . . . 1 medium . . . . 15 g
Persimmon . . . . 1 . . . . 8 g
Physalis . . . . 1 . . . . trace
Pineapple . . . . 1 slice . . . . 15 g
Plum . . . . 1 small . . . . 2 g
Plum . . . . 1 large . . . . 7 g
Pomegranate . . . . 1 medium . . . . 15 g
Prune . . . . 1 . . . . 3 g
Raisins . . . . small handful . . . . 10 g
Raspberries . . . . 3 heaped tbsp . . . . 5 g
Satsuma . . . . 1 . . . . 5 g
Starfruit . . . . 1 . . . . 7 g
Strawberries, sliced . . . . 3 heaped tbsp . . . . 6 g
Sultanas (golden raisins) . . . . small handful . . . . 10 g

Vegetables
Check the list on pages 11–12 and add your extra carbohydrates for Phase 2 from a variety of vegetables.

Other foods
You may also include any from the following list. However,
don't confuse wild rice with wild rice mix, which is half long-
grain white rice and so has a much higher carb content. Full-
fat soya flour is much lower in carbs than wheat or other grain
flours, so is good for baking.

Item	Quantity	Carb content
Crispbread, rye	1 slice	6 g
Crispbread, starch-reduced	1 slice	3 g
Crispbread, wheat	1 slice	7 g
Crisp rice cakes	1	7 g
Fortified unsweetened soya milk	300 ml/½ pt/ 1¼ cups	2 g
Full-fat soya flour	4 tbsp	6 g
Greek-style strained yoghurt made with cow's milk	100 ml/3½ fl oz/ scant ½ cup	4 g
Sauerkraut	3 heaped tbsp	5 g
Soya beans (soaked and cooked)	3 heaped tbsp	5 g
Wild rice, uncooked	50 g/2 oz/¼ cup	6 g

Side dishes and other 10 g options

Other ways to add some carefully controlled extra carbs are to serve a side dish or drink with your main meal or enjoy a tasty snack. Any of these suggestions will give you an extra 10 g of carbohydrate.

- 1 tumbler (250 ml/8 fl oz/1 cup) of pure apple juice
- 1 cream cracker or water biscuit with cheese and 5 ml/1 tsp sweet pickle or chutney
- 1 taco shell with grated cheese, 1 sliced tomato, a handful of shredded lettuce and 5 slices of cucumber

- 1 starch-reduced bread roll, buttered if liked
- 1 rollmop herring, sliced, on 1 buttered starch-reduced crispbread
- 10 sticks of cheese and pineapple
- 100 g/4 oz/3 heaped tbsp cooked fresh shelled or frozen peas
- 1 medium cooked beetroot (red beet), with or without vinegar
- 100 g/4 oz/3 heaped tbsp cooked soya beans and 1 diced green (bell) pepper, in mayonnaise or oil and vinegar dressing, flavoured with snipped chives

Side dishes and other 15 g options
Once you are adding up to 15 g of carbohydrate, you have even more choice. Here's some 11–15 g ideas.
- 100 g/4 oz/3 heaped tbsp cooked, frozen broad (fava) beans
- 100 g/4 oz/3 heaped tbsp Jerusalem artichokes, mashed or puréed with butter or cream
- 100 g/4 oz/3 heaped tbsp parsnips, mashed, with butter if liked
- 100 g/4 oz/3 heaped tbsp ratatouille
- 1 small or ½ large corn-on-the-cob, with melted butter if liked
- 100 g/4 oz/3 heaped tbsp canned fruit in natural juice
- 125 ml/4½ oz/1 small pot of Greek-style yoghurt with honey
- 300 ml/½ pt/1¼ cups cow's milk

Phase 3: Building Towards a Normal Healthy Diet

By the time you reach this phase, you will have lost most of the weight you want to shed. This phase is designed to help you start to look towards a long-term eating plan by introducing a few treats, such as a small jacket potato or a slice of bread – the kind of thing that we all like to eat when we are 'eating normally'. This is what the diet is intended to do – it offers you a way to eat those 'normal' foods, while still checking that your weight continues to fall, albeit more slowly now.

During Phase 3, you should continue to maintain the same carbohydrate intake that you had reached at the end of Phase 2. But now, two or three times a week, you can introduce one of the higher-carbohydrate 'treats' (see pages 26–28). Take note of their carbohydrate content and continue to monitor your weight weekly. If you start gaining weight, reduce the number of treats. On the other hand, if you're still losing quickly, you can have an extra treat or two. Alternatively, you can have additional carbohydrates from the lists of those already allowed. Just make a note of what carbohydrates you've eaten, so you can increase or decrease accordingly.

The treats

You'll see that some of these treats are highly nutritious, but many are purely for indulgence. They all have 15 g of carbs, or fewer. If you find you start to gain weight with this level of treats, cut them back again. It's up to you to manage your body according to its metabolism.

You can put two treats together in one meal, such as a slice of toast with butter and marmalade, but make sure you remember that you've had two-in-one!

Two or three times a week add any of the following:

- 100 g/4 oz new or old potatoes, steamed, boiled or mashed (with butter or margarine if liked) or a small jacket potato (with butter or margarine, grated cheese, crème fraîche and chive dressing or mayonnaise).
- A portion of crispy potato skins. Scrub your potatoes, then peel them and put the peelings on a baking (cookie) sheet. Bake in the oven at 200°C/400°F/gas 6/fan oven 180°C for about 20 minutes until crisp and golden. Season lightly with salt and pepper and leave to cool. Store in an airtight container for a few days, if necessary. This delicious, nutritious snack has only 7 g of carbohydrates per medium potato, so you can have up to 2 potatoes-worth per serving.

Note: Peeled potatoes can also be stored covered with water in an airtight container in the fridge for up to 24 hours. Drain and cook in fresh water.

- 1 thin slice of bread (preferably wholemeal) from a large sliced loaf, with butter if liked
- 1 medium slice of an uncut loaf such as a bloomer, with butter if liked
- 1 slice of currant bread, with butter if liked
- 1 crumpet, with butter or margarine if liked
- A portion of gnocchi, with butter and Parmesan cheese if liked
- 2 small slices of garlic bread
- 1 individual Yorkshire pudding
- 1 Weetabix or Shredded Wheat, with unsweetened fortified soya milk
- 2 heaped tbsp cooked couscous or bulghar (cracked wheat)
- 3 heaped tbsp cooked dried peas, beans or lentils
- 2 plain biscuits (cookies) or 1 biscuit half-coated in chocolate
- 2 sponge (lady) fingers
- ½ standard bar of chocolate or 1 fun-size bar
- 1 scoop of ice cream
- 1 tbsp (2 tbsp if reduced-sugar) jam (conserve), marmalade or honey
- 1 small bag of potato crisps (chips)
- 1 onion bhaji or pakora
- 2 popadoms
- 1 small pancake roll
- 1 meat samosa
- 1 potato waffle

- 1 hash brown
- 5 deep-fried onion rings
- 1 pancake, with lemon and sugar
- 1 pint of beer
- ½ pint of medium-sweet cider
- 1 double measure (50 ml/2 fl oz) of sweet vermouth or sherry
- 2 glasses of Sangria
- 1 lemonade shandy
- 1 sweetened speciality coffee, such as Gaelic coffee

Slipping back

Because you can now have treats, it is very easy to think 'An extra bar of chocolate won't hurt' – and on its own it probably wouldn't. The trouble is, before you know it, this will become a habit, and you'll have started eating cakes, chocolates, sweets (candies), sugary desserts – the lot! Having trained your body so well for so long, you shouldn't throw it all away now. Remember, treats really should be treats and that means only a couple of times a week.

Phase 4: Maintaining the New You

Congratulations – you've reached your goal! Now you are the weight or size you want to be. Your diet should now include lots of fruit and vegetables, and a certain amount of starchy foods like bread, potatoes, rice and pasta. However, you should go easy on butter, cream and other fatty foods. I prefer to use low-fat alternatives like reduced-fat olive or sunflower oil spread, crème fraîche and yoghurts. Yes, they do contain more carbohydrates than full-fat alternatives but, long-term, they are better for your cholesterol levels. As so often in life, moderation is the key to success. Now you can eat a little of almost anything you like (though I would prefer that you eat wholegrain products and give processed foods a miss most of the time). But you must continue to keep an eye on how much carbohydrate you eat, particularly keeping cakes, biscuits and other sugary foods for treats and special occasions.

Every day, enjoy the recipes from this book – or other low-carbohydrate meals of your choice, but include a small portion of carbohydrate, such as 2 tablespoons of rice with your beef stroganoff or just a few baby new potatoes with your salmon salad.

Weigh yourself each week. If you find you start to gain weight again, simply cut back on the extra starchy carbohydrates. You'll soon get used to managing your eating long-term. That doesn't mean you can't ever over-indulge. That would be awful! So if, for instance, you go out to an Italian restaurant and tuck into a large bowl of creamy risotto and a plate of garlic bread, followed by some rich chocolate dessert, don't worry – simply have a very low-carb day the next day. It's not about fanaticism; it's about balance.

Hidden carbohydrates

We all know that carbohydrates are contained in starchy foods like bread, pasta, rice and potatoes, and that sugars are found in sweet things like fruit, cakes, chocolate, biscuits (cookies), sweets (candies) and ice cream. But carbohydrates are found in lots of other foods that may surprise you. Always read the labels when shopping so that you can make informed choices. Most important, be wary of any food that claims to be 'low-fat' or 'light': these will nearly always have added starches or sugars to compensate for the reduced amount of fat.

Meats, seafood and poultry with hidden carbs
- Some delicatessen meats
- Processed meat products such as sausages, frankfurters, pâtés and potted meats
- Crab sticks and other imitation fish products

- Fish fingers and pastes; canned fish in sauce
- Shaped chicken and turkey fingers, drumsticks, etc.
  Note: Some offal and fish contain small amounts of carbohydrates naturally.

Dairy products with hidden carbs
- Milk
- Yoghurts (especially the low-fat and fat-free thick ones, which have starchy fillers)
- Cheese spread
- Dried milk (non-fat dry milk)
  Note: Fresh soft cheeses have more carbohydrates in the lower-fat versions.

Sauces, dressings and condiments with hidden carbs
Many have sugar and/or starch added. You may expect these in pickles and chutneys, but they turn up in some unexpected places, so read the labels on everything, including the following:
- Tomato ketchup (catsup)
- Commercial salad cream
- Bought French dressing
- Blended spices and baking powder, which may contain starchy fillers
- Garlic purée (paste)
- Speciality vinegars
- Mustards

- Soy sauce
- Coffee whitener
- Stock cubes

Drinks with hidden carbs
- Coffee and cocoa contain some carbohydrates
- Beers, sweet wines and liqueurs are high in carbohydrates
- Watch out for diet drinks. Unless they are labelled as containing 0 calories, they will, probably, contain some carbs. Always check the labels and be sensible. You will note that in a few recipes I have called for sugar-free real blackcurrant cordial. Undiluted, it has 0.5 g carbohydrates per 30 ml/2 tbsp, so a tablespoonful isn't going to make much difference to your carbohydrate intake in a day. But, if you were to drink, say, 10 small glasses in a day, that would be an extra 5 g of carbohydrates. If you had large glasses, it could amount to as much as 10 g.

Healthy Eating on a Low-carbohydrate Diet

Before you begin

It is important that you check with your doctor that you are fit and will not suffer any health problems by embarking on a low-carbohydrate diet. If, for instance, you are already on a low-fat regime, or on a low-cholesterol diet for medical reasons, it may not be suitable for you to go on a low-carbohydrate diet. In particular, if you are diabetic, it is very unlikely that this type of diet would be suitable for you as it would be almost impossible to keep your blood sugar levels low and stable.

The five food groups

You have to understand what your body needs to stay fit and healthy throughout your life.

Although you are about to embark on a different regime from that generally considered to be normal for a healthy lifestyle, it is possible to eat a balanced diet for ever on a lower-than-usual carbohydrate intake and therefore maintain a slim figure and a healthy body. What you must never do is simply cut out carbohydrates – or any other food group for that matter. If you do you will become ill, so don't even consider it.

Cutting down carbohydrates drastically for the first two weeks of the diet for quick weight loss is perfectly acceptable but you should not do it any longer than that. Your body needs nutrients from all the food groups to maintain health and vitality, and so any diet – even a weight-reducing one – should include reasonable proportions of all the main food groups.

Proteins

These are used by the body for growth and repair and, when necessary, for energy. The best sources are fish, lean meat, poultry, dairy products, eggs, soya proteins such as tofu, and Quorn, which is made from a fungus. Pulses – dried peas, beans and lentils – are good sources too, but they are also high in carbohydrates, so only eat them later on in the diet and in limited quantities. When on a low-carbohydrate diet, you should eat more proteins than usual in order to maintain the energy levels that your body needs. However, when you start increasing your carbohydrates, you should reduce your protein level slightly or you'll end up eating too much overall.

A note about eggs too. Because they are a high-protein food they are used a lot on a low-carb diet and you are likely to eat quite a few in the first two weeks of dieting. However, long-term, it is recommended you don't have more than three or four in any week, so bear that in mind when you are planning you meals, especially when you get to the maintenance stage.

Carbohydrates

There are two types of carbohydrate. Complex carbohydrates are all the starchy foods such as bread, pasta, rice, cereals (including breakfast cereals) and tubers such as potatoes. Simple carbohydrates are sugars and include those naturally found in foods – like fructose in fruit and lactose in milk – as well as refined sugars used in cakes, biscuits (cookies) and sweets (candies). Nutritionally, the starchy ones and the natural sugars in milk, fruit, etc., are usually considered 'good' foods and are used by the body for energy. Refined sugars contain only empty calories, that is they do not contain any valuable nutrients, and should be avoided.

On a weight-reducing, low-carbohydrate plan, this food group is radically reduced in the first phase of the diet, but then re-introduced slowly, in limited quantities. The body cannot function properly without carbohydrates in the long term so don't keep them at a drastically low level for more than the first two weeks of the diet.

Vitamins and minerals

These are vital for general health and well-being. Many vitamins and minerals are found in fruit and vegetables. Choose fresh, frozen or those that are canned in water or natural juice with no added sugar – and, ideally, no added salt. It is recommended that everyone eats at least five portions a day.

35

When you begin your low-carb diet, fruit and vegetables have to be very restricted. However, this severely limited phase is very short and as you progress you should eat more and a greater variety. It is essential that you eat all those suggested in any recipe because they are vital to your health. If you don't like a particular one, substitute another with the same carbohydrate count from the lists on pages 11–13 and 20–22. I also recommend you take a good-quality vitamin and mineral supplement daily, although do check that it contains no sugar or starch.

Fats

Like carbohydrates, fats can be converted by the body into energy and are also used for warmth. They are found naturally in foods high in protein – such as dairy products, meat, fish, poultry, nuts, seeds and some fruits, particularly olives and avocados (which makes these a bonus on a low-carb plan).

A low-carbohydrate diet may include some fat – and fat is actually essential for your body to function properly. However, large amounts of animal fat can cause heart problems and strokes, so don't overdo your intake of butter and cream (I recommend having olive and sunflower oils and spreads instead) and choose lean meats wherever possible.

Fibre

Fibre is not a food group as such but it is vital for healthy body functioning. Lack of fibre will make your digestion – and you – sluggish and may lead to other health problems.

While on your low-carb diet, you should make sure you eat lots of dark green vegetables and lots of nuts and seeds, once these are allowed. Drink plenty of water and take plenty of exercise to help prevent constipation. When you are allowed to have potatoes and fruits such as apples, eat the skin as well. If you do find you are becoming constipated, linseed sprinkled on your salad or fruit is particularly helpful.

Fluids

Whether you are dieting or not, your body needs a minimum of 2 litres (3½ pints) of fluid a day. Drink lots of water – from the tap, filtered, mineral or no-calorie flavoured waters – and make up the remainder with hot or cold drinks.

Low-carb dieters may wish to avoid caffeine (contained in tea, coffee, hot chocolate, cola, etc.) because it may trigger the production of insulin and so impair weight loss (see How a Low-carbohydrate Diet Works, pages 6–7). I suggest that you drink weak black tea or coffee at first (add cream, not milk, if you like it white, then later fortified unsweetened soya milk, which is much lower in carbohydrates than cow's milk). Alternatively, choose caffeine-free ones or try herbal teas. I would stress, though, that coffee and cocoa contain small amounts of carbohydrate, so if you drink a lot you have to include them in your counting; tea has none. You may also have no-carbohydrate (diet) soft drinks, carbohydrate-free clear soups, and pure lemon or lime juice well diluted with water and artificially sweetened, if necessary. (There is a trace of carbohydrate in them but not as much as in other fruit juices.)

Do not drink milk or sweet pure fruit juices until well into your diet and do include them in your carbohydrate count. Never have soft drinks sweetened with sugar.

Alcohol

Only some types of alcohol are allowed.

- You may have dry red wine and spirits as they have only a trace of carbohydrate. Remember, though, that your body can derive energy easily from alcohol, so it will burn that before any fat. Ideally, avoid alcohol for the first two weeks.
- Always have no-calorie mixers with spirits.
- Drink plenty of water before and after drinking alcohol. Eat foods high in protein when drinking alcohol so that the body will process them together.
- Dry white, rosé and dry fortified wines have 1–2 g of carbohydrate per average glass so should not be included early on in this diet.
- Avoid beers, sweet wines, sweet fortified wines and liqueurs as they are high in carbohydrates.

Notes on the Recipes

- Ingredients are given in metric, imperial and American measures. Follow one set only. American terms are in brackets.
- The ingredients are listed in the order in which they are used.
- All spoon measures are level unless otherwise stated: 1 tsp = 5 ml; 1 tbsp = 15 ml.
- Eggs and whole vegetables or fruit are medium unless stated.
- Wash, peel, core and seed, if necessary, fresh produce.
- Seasoning and the use of strongly flavoured ingredients are very much a matter of personal taste. Use less than recommended if you prefer. Keep salt to a minimum.
- Always use fresh herbs unless dried are specified. If you substitute dried for fresh, use only half the quantity or less. Frozen, chopped varieties have a better colour and flavour than the dried ones.
- All can and packet sizes are approximate.
- In some cases I have given a suggested size for pieces of meat, fish or chicken. More or less won't affect your carbohydrate counts – but don't be greedy!
- Cooking times are approximate and should be used as a guide only. Food should be piping hot and cooked through.
- It is not necessary to preheat a fan oven and the food can be placed on any of the shelves. Conventional ovens should be

preheated and the food placed on the shelf just above the centre unless otherwise stated.

- Most of the dishes serve four people but can easily be halved or quartered, if necessary, to serve two or one.

- Remember to check the carbohydrate content of everything from stock cubes to calorie-free drinks – but don't become obsessive. For instance, a stock cube may contain 1.2 g carbohydrate but you'd only use the whole cube in a recipe for four, which makes it low in carbohydrate per portion.

- Granular artificial sweetener is only a tenth of the weight of ordinary sugar, so never try to weigh it: measure it by volume only (e.g. spoon or cup measures). Also note that, if overheated, it can taste bitter. If you want to add extra to a recipe, do so a little at a time.

- I have called for butter in the recipes but there is no reason why you shouldn't use margarine if you prefer. Note, however, that low-fat varieties tend to be higher in carbohydrates and that some margarines are not suitable for cooking. Check the labels on both points.

- You can personalise recipes by substituting ingredients. If they contain carbs, make sure you exchange like for like.

- I have used alcohol in some of the recipes. However, it will not affect your diet either because the quantity is too small or because it is cooked, so that it has already evaporated.

- If you are concerned that caffeine may slow your weight loss, use decaffeinated coffee in recipes and for drinking.

Breakfast Recipes

All these recipes make the perfect start to the day. Some are quick and easy for when you have to dash out to work, others are best eaten and enjoyed at your leisure. You can, if you must, have eggs and bacon every morning instead – but if you do I would recommend grilling the bacon and poaching the eggs most of the time, as large quantities of fried foods aren't good for anyone!

Golden soufflé omelette

Light and delicious, this makes a perfect start to the day. The flavour is heightened with fragrant herbs and you could add a handful of grated Cheddar cheese or diced ham too, if you like.

SERVES 1
CARBOHYDRATES: 0 G

2 eggs, separated
10 ml/2 tsp water
Salt and freshly ground black pepper
5 ml/1 tsp chopped fresh parsley
A good pinch of dried mixed herbs
15 g/½ oz/1 tbsp butter

1 Beat the egg yolks and water together with a little salt and pepper. Stir in the fresh and dried herbs.

2 Whisk the egg whites until stiff and fold into the yolk mixture with a metal spoon.

3 Melt the butter in an omelette pan. When hot, spoon in the soufflé mixture and spread it out evenly. Cook gently for about 3–4 minutes until golden underneath and partially set. Meanwhile, preheat the grill (broiler).

4 Put the omelette in its pan under the grill and cook until puffy and golden brown. Serve immediately.

Pan-scrambled eggs with smoked salmon

This dish is equally delicious made with a handful of smoked diced ham instead of the salmon. Either way it makes a really sumptuous breakfast so you can treat yourself any day!

SERVES 4

CARBOHYDRATES: 0 G PER SERVING ❶

100 g/4 oz smoked salmon trimmings
8 eggs
120 ml/4 fl oz/½ cup water
Salt and freshly ground black pepper
25 g/1 oz/2 tbsp butter
60 ml/4 tbsp chopped fresh parsley

1 Cut up any larger bits of salmon and separate them if they're stuck together. Set aside.

2 Beat the eggs with the water, a pinch of salt and a good grinding of pepper.

3 Melt the butter in a frying pan (skillet). Add the eggs and sprinkle the parsley over. Cook over a fairly gentle heat, stirring occasionally, until they just begin to scramble.

4 Scatter the salmon all over the surface of the egg and continue to cook, stirring all the time, until the eggs are scrambled. Tip on to warm plates and serve.

Grilled kippers with creamy scrambled eggs

Kippers make a perfect accompaniment to soft, lightly cooked scrambled eggs. If you don't like kippers, you can substitute smoked mackerel or bacon, or make extra scrambled eggs.

SERVES 4

CARBOHYDRATES: TRACE PER SERVING

4 kippers, on the bone or filleted

50 g/2 oz/¼ cup butter

8 eggs

120 ml/4 fl oz/½ cup double (heavy) cream

Salt and freshly ground black pepper

1 Put the kippers skin-side up on foil on the grill (broiler) rack. Grill (broil) for 2 minutes. Turn the fish over and dot with half the butter. Grill for a further 2–3 minutes until cooked through and sizzling.

2 Meanwhile, melt the remaining butter in a non-stick saucepan. Whisk in the eggs, cream and a little salt and pepper. Cook over a gentle heat, stirring all the time, until scrambled but still creamy.

3 Transfer the fish and eggs to warm plates and serve.

Giant stuffed mushrooms with ham and cheese

Enormous mushrooms cradling slices of lean cured ham, lifted with just a dash of Worcestershire sauce and smothered in mild Edam cheese – this is good enough for any time of day.

SERVES 4

CARBOHYDRATES: 1 G PER SERVING ❶

8 very large open-cup mushrooms
60 ml/4 tbsp olive oil
Freshly ground black pepper
8 slices of ham
A few drops of Worcestershire sauce
100 g/4 oz/1 cup grated Edam cheese

1 Peel the mushrooms and trim off the stalks. Brush all over with the oil and sprinkle with lots of pepper.

2 Place gill-sides down on foil on the grill (broiler) rack. Cook under a preheated grill for 3 minutes until turning golden.

3 Turn the mushrooms over and place a slice of ham in each mushroom, folding it to fit. Sprinkle each with a few drops of Worcestershire sauce, then top with the cheese. Grill (broil) for a further 3 minutes until the cheese melts and bubbles.

4 Slide on to warm plates and pour any juices over.

Poached eggs with spinach and creamed mushrooms

A gourmet breakfast of softly poached eggs set on lightly cooked, tender young spinach coated in a creamy mushroom sauce – a wonderful combination of textures and flavours.

SERVES 4

CARBOHYDRATES: 1 G PER SERVING

A knob of butter

225 g/8 oz button mushrooms, thinly sliced

120 ml/4 fl oz/½ cup crème fraîche

A good pinch of onion salt

Freshly ground black pepper

450 g/1 lb fresh young spinach

8 eggs

60 ml/4 tbsp lemon juice or vinegar

1 Melt the butter in a saucepan. Add the mushrooms and cook, stirring, for 2 minutes. Stir in the crème fraîche and season with the onion salt and lots of pepper.

2 Wash the spinach thoroughly and place in a saucepan with no extra water. Cover and cook over a gentle heat, stirring once or twice, for 3 minutes until just softened but not mushy. Drain thoroughly.

3 Meanwhile, poach the eggs in simmering water with the lemon juice or vinegar added for 3–4 minutes until cooked to your liking. (You can use an egg poacher if you prefer.)

4 Reheat the mushrooms. Put the spinach on warm plates, top with the eggs and spoon the creamed mushrooms over.

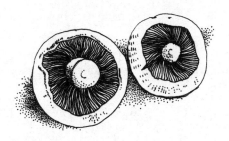

Grilled halloumi with bacon

A touch of the Mediterranean here – slices of firm, slightly salty Halloumi cheese, drizzled with olive oil, spiked with lemon and oregano and grilled until golden with smoked bacon.

SERVES 4
CARBOHYDRATES: 1 G PER SERVING

1 block of Halloumi cheese, cut into 12 slices
60 ml/4 tbsp olive oil
1 lemon, quartered
Dried oregano
Freshly ground black pepper
8 rashers (slices) of smoked back bacon, rinded

1 Put the cheese on foil on a grill (broiler) rack and drizzle with the oil. Squeeze the lemon over, then sprinkle each slice with a pinch of oregano and lots of pepper. Lay the bacon alongside.

2 Cook under a preheated grill for 3–4 minutes until the cheese and bacon are lightly golden. If you haven't room for the bacon and cheese on your grill at the same time, either fry (sauté) the bacon in a frying pan (skillet) while you cook the cheese, or grill (broil) the cheese, transfer it to a plate and keep it warm in a low oven while grilling the bacon.

3 Transfer the cheese and bacon to warm plates and serve.

Devilled kidneys with mushrooms

A taste of the old days! Succulent kidneys spiked with spices and bathed in a rich sauce – a substantial breakfast to enjoy at your leisure and set you up for the rest of the day.

SERVES 4

CARBOHYDRATES: 2 G PER SERVING ❶

8 lambs' kidneys
100 g/4 oz/½ cup butter
5 ml/1 tsp chilli powder
5 ml/1 tsp made English mustard
5 ml/1 tsp paprika
60 ml/4 tbsp tomato purée (paste)
Salt and freshly ground black pepper
Artificial sweetener, to taste
225 g/8 oz button mushrooms, halved or quartered

1 Remove any skin from the kidneys and snip out the central cores with scissors. Cut the kidneys into bite-sized pieces.

2 Melt the butter in a frying pan (skillet). Add the kidneys and fry (sauté), stirring, for 3 minutes until brown but still soft.

3 Add the chilli, mustard, paprika and tomato purée and stir until thoroughly blended. Season to taste with salt, pepper and sweetener. Simmer for 1–2 minutes, stirring.

4 Spoon into warm shallow bowls and serve with the raw mushrooms to mop up the juices.

49

Victorian-style mumbled eggs with cream cheese

An old-fashioned recipe that was created when people took time over their breakfasts. They're too good to rush so sit down and really relish the subtle flavours at your leisure.

SERVES 4

CARBOHYDRATES: 2 G PER SERVING

4 tomatoes, sliced
120 ml/4 fl oz/½ cup whipping cream
100 g/4 oz/½ cup cream cheese
8 eggs
10 ml/2 tsp made English mustard
Salt and freshly ground black pepper

1 Arrange the tomato slices in a circle on four plates. Place in a very low oven to warm.

2 Put the cream and cheese in a saucepan and heat gently, stirring until smooth.

3 Remove from the heat and whisk in the eggs, mustard and a little salt and pepper. Return to the heat and cook gently, stirring, until just set but still creamy.

4 Spoon into the centres of the tomato rings and serve.

Baked eggs in tomatoes with cheese

Large juicy tomatoes make perfect nests for eggs, topped with golden, melted cheese. I like to use Cheddar, but you can experiment with other favourites for a change.

SERVES 4
CARBOHYDRATES: 4 G PER SERVING

4 large beefsteak tomatoes
A little olive oil
8 smallish eggs
Freshly ground black pepper
100 g/4 oz/1 cup grated Cheddar cheese

1 Preheat the oven to 180°C/350°F/gas 4/fan oven 160°C. Halve the tomatoes and scoop out the seeds.

2 Stand two half tomato shells in each of four lightly oiled individual dishes and brush inside with olive oil.

3 Break an egg into each tomato half, season with pepper, then top with the cheese.

4 Bake in the oven for 12–15 minutes for soft-cooked eggs, 20 minutes if you like the yolks hard.

Home-made sausages with tomatoes

If you are eating alone, freeze the remaining uncooked sausages or store them in the fridge for up to three days. They contain no carbs – but do eat only two tomatoes.

SERVES 4

CARBOHYDRATES: 4 G PER SERVING

450 g/1 lb belly pork slices
225 g/8 oz bacon pieces
5 ml/1 tsp dried mixed herbs
Freshly ground black pepper
8 tomatoes, halved
Olive oil

1   Cut the rind off the belly pork slices and cut out any bones. Cut into chunks.

2   Pick over the bacon, discarding any bones, gristle or rind. Cut into smaller pieces, if necessary.

3   Drop the pork and bacon a piece at a time into a food processor with the machine running until finely chopped, or pass through a mincer (grinder). Season with the herbs and lots of pepper.

4 Draw the mixture together into a ball. Remove any white stringy bits of gristly pork fat that haven't chopped. Shape the mixture into small sausages or balls.

5 Place the sausages and tomato halves on foil on a grill (broiler) rack. Drizzle the tomatoes with a little olive oil. Grill (broil) for about 5–6 minutes, turning the sausages occasionally, until golden and cooked through. Turn the tomatoes once. Alternatively, fry (sauté) the sausages and tomatoes in a little olive oil for a similar length of time.

6 Transfer the sausages and tomatoes to warm plates and serve.

Celeriac and onion hash browns with bacon

Traditional hash browns are a no-no as they contain potato but my mouthwatering morsels, made with elegant celeriac, are a fabulous low-carb alternative. They're delicious hot or cold.

SERVES 4
CARBOHYDRATES: 7 G PER SERVING

❶

1 celeriac (celery root), cut into small chunks
8 rashers (slices) of back bacon, rinded
60 ml/4 tbsp sunflower or olive oil
2 onions, chopped
Salt and freshly ground black pepper
2 eggs, beaten
25 g/1 oz/2 tbsp butter

1 Boil the celeriac in lightly salted water for about 10 minutes until soft. Drain and tip into a bowl. Mash well.

2 Meanwhile, fry (sauté) the bacon in a frying pan (skillet) until golden, turning once. Remove from the pan and keep warm.

3 Add half the oil to the pan and heat. Add the onion and fry for 2 minutes, stirring.

4 Remove from the pan with a draining spoon and add to the celeriac. Mix together well, season with salt and pepper, then mix in the beaten eggs.

5 Add the butter and the remaining oil to the frying pan. Heat until bubbling, swirling the pan to blend the fats together, then add spoonfuls of the celeriac mixture and fry for 2 minutes until golden underneath. Turn the hash browns over and fry the other sides until golden. If necessary, cook in two batches and keep the first batch warm while cooking the remainder.

6 Drain on kitchen paper (paper towels), then serve with the bacon.

Top tip
If you are cooking for one, it's still worth cooking the whole celeriac. You can keep it in the fridge for a few days, or freeze it to use at a later date.

Lunch Recipes

The recipes in this section make tasty light meals that you can enjoy with a slice of Low-carbohydrate Soya Bread (only 2 g carb per slice, see page 102) or a breadstick (3 g carb). Alternatively team one of the soups with a no-carb or very low-carb starter or snack from pages 80–96.

Fresh sherried chicken broth with herbs

You can also make this delicious clear soup with a cooked chicken carcass. If you need only one serving, the rest can be stored in the fridge for several days, or frozen in portions.

SERVES 4
CARBOHYDRATES: TRACE PER SERVING

1 chicken leg portion
1 onion, washed and quartered but not peeled
1 celery stick, chopped
1 bouquet garni sachet
1 chicken stock cube
1 litre/1¾ pts/4¼ cups water
Salt and freshly ground black pepper
45 ml/3 tbsp dry sherry

1 Put all the ingredients except the sherry in a saucepan. Bring to the boil and skim the surface.

2 Reduce the heat, cover and simmer very gently for 1½ hours. Strain, then return it to the rinsed-out saucepan.

3 When cool enough to handle, pick all the meat off the bones, discarding the skin. Chop the flesh and return it to the pan. Stir in the sherry. Taste and re-season, if necessary.

4 Reheat and serve hot.

Caesar salad with anchovies and crispy bacon

Crisp lettuce and crunchy bacon tossed in a garlic and anchovy dressing, then topped with fresh Parmesan. Leftover anchovies can be stored in the fridge for several days or frozen for later use.

SERVES 4

CARBOHYDRATES: 2 G PER SERVING

❶

2 × 50 g/2 oz/small cans of anchovies
8 rashers (slices) of streaky bacon, rinded and diced
1 small cos (romaine) lettuce, cut into chunks
2 large eggs
1 garlic clove, crushed
175 ml/6 fl oz/¾ cup sunflower oil
60 ml/4 tbsp white wine vinegar
10 ml/2 tsp Dijon mustard
10 ml/2 tsp artificial sweetener
Salt and freshly ground black pepper
100 g/4 oz/1 cup freshly shaved Parmesan cheese

1 Put the anchovies in a small bowl. Cover with cold water and leave to soak while preparing the rest of the salad.

2 Dry-fry the bacon in a frying pan (skillet) until crisp and golden. Drain on kitchen paper (paper towels).

3 Put the prepared lettuce in a bowl and sprinkle with the fried bacon.

4 Put the eggs in a pan of cold water. Bring to the boil and boil for just 1½ minutes – no longer – then plunge them immediately into cold water.

5 Drain the anchovies and chop four of them. Put in a bowl with the garlic and work together with a wire whisk.

6 Break the eggs into the bowl. Whisk into the anchovy mixture, then whisk in the oil a drop at a time until thick. Finally, add the vinegar, mustard, sweetener and salt and pepper to taste.

7 Cut the remaining anchovies into two or three pieces and add to the lettuce. Pour the dressing over and toss. Scatter with the Parmesan shavings and serve.

Tuna mornay with roasted peanuts

A sizzling blend of tuna, peanuts and cheese. Buying this size can of tuna is more economical so, if eating alone, make half the quantity and have the remainder cold or microwaved the next day.

SERVES 4
CARBOHYDRATES: 3 G PER SERVING

2 × 185 g/6½ oz/small cans of tuna, drained
100 g/4 oz/1 cup roasted peanuts
150 ml/¼ pt/⅔ cup crème fraîche
150 ml/¼ pt/⅔ cup water
2 eggs, beaten
Freshly ground black pepper
5 ml/1 tsp dried mixed herbs
100 g/4 oz/1 cup grated Cheddar cheese
30 ml/2 tbsp chopped fresh parsley

1 Empty the tuna into a shallow ovenproof dish and mix in the nuts.

2 Beat together the crème fraîche, water and eggs with some black pepper and the dried herbs. Spoon the crème fraîche mixture over the tuna and peanuts and sprinkle the cheese liberally over the surface.

3 Bake in a preheated oven at 190°C/375°F/gas 5/fan oven 170°C for about 30 minutes until just set, golden and bubbling.

4 Sprinkle with the parsley and serve hot.

Top tip
A simple tomato salad, dressed with oil, vinegar, a pinch of artificial sweetener and some salt and pepper (4 g carb for 2 tomatoes) would go well with this recipe.

Curried egg mayonnaise with cucumber and watercress

A tasty long-time favourite. Halve the quantity of eggs and dressing (0 g carbs) for a small appetite.

SERVES 4

CARBOHYDRATES: 3 G PER SERVING

8 eggs
4 good handfuls of torn lettuce
4 good handfuls of trimmed watercress
10 cm/4 in piece of cucumber, diced
5 ml/1 tsp curry powder
120 ml/4 fl oz/½ cup mayonnaise
10 ml/2 tsp lemon juice
Artificial sweetener, to taste
A pinch of dried parsley, to garnish

1   Put the eggs in a pan of cold water, bring to the boil and boil for 7 minutes. Drain, cover with cold water and leave until cold. Shell and halve the eggs.

2   Mix together the lettuce and watercress and pile on to four plates. Scatter the cucumber over. Arrange the eggs on top.

3   Blend the curry powder with the mayonnaise, lemon juice and sweetener to taste. Spoon over the eggs and dust with a little dried parsley.

Cheese-stuffed eggs with mixed green salad

This is a deliciously simple lunch dish: hard-boiled egg yolk blended with blue cheese, mayonnaise and black pepper, then piled into the egg whites and served on a bed of salad.

SERVES 4
CARBOHYDRATES: 3 G PER SERVING

❶

4 hard-boiled (hard-cooked) eggs
100 g/4 oz soft blue cheese
60 ml/4 tbsp mayonnaise
Freshly ground black pepper
4 good handfuls of mixed salad leaves
1 green (bell) pepper, thinly sliced
10 cm/4 in piece of cucumber, thinly sliced
1 box of salad cress

1　Shell the eggs and cut into halves. Scoop out the yolks into a bowl. Mash well with the cheese and mayonnaise, then season with pepper to taste.

2　Pile the cheese mixture back into the hollows of the egg white halves.

3　Arrange the salad leaves, pepper and cucumber on four plates. Top with the stuffed eggs and add a cluster of cress between the egg halves.

Clear mixed winter vegetable soup

This is a brilliant way to get a good portion of your five-a-day vegetables in one bowl! It's filling, colourful and very nutritious – and exceptionally tasty into the bargain.

SERVES 4
CARBOHYDRATES: 4 G PER SERVING

❶

1 carrot, coarsely grated
1 turnip, coarsely grated
¼ head of celeriac (celery root), coarsely grated
1 litre/1¾ pts/4¼ cups vegetable stock,
made with 1½ stock cubes
2.5 ml/½ tsp Marmite or other yeast extract
1 bay leaf
Freshly ground black pepper

1 Put all the ingredients in a saucepan. Bring to the boil, reduce the heat, part-cover and simmer for 10 minutes.

2 Remove the bay leaf and season with more pepper, if necessary. Ladle into warm bowls to serve.

Chilled cream of cucumber soup with dill

Cool, refreshing and revitalising – just three adjectives to describe this delicious Mediterranean-style chilled soup. It makes a perfect lunch dish, especially on a hot day.

SERVES 4

CARBOHYDRATES: 4 G PER SERVING

❶

1 cucumber
Salt
10 ml/2 tsp dried dill (dill weed)
30 ml/2 tbsp white wine vinegar
300 ml/½ pt/1¼ cups crème fraîche
Freshly ground black pepper
300 ml/½ pt/1¼ cups cold water

1 Coarsely grate the cucumber into a colander. Sprinkle well with salt and leave to stand for 10 minutes. Rinse with cold water, then squeeze out all the moisture.

2 Tip the cucumber into a bowl and stir in the dill, wine vinegar, crème fraîche and a good grinding of pepper.

3 Chill the soup, if time allows, although this is not essential.

4 When ready to serve, stir in the cold water, taste and adjust the seasoning, if necessary.

Salmon mousse with artichoke and watercress

This delicately flavoured mousse tastes as good as any made with fresh salmon! The mousse has no carbs at all, so you can indulge yourself and have a larger portion if you wish.

SERVES 4
CARBOHYDRATES: 4 G PER SERVING

1 × 400 g/14 oz/large can of red or pink salmon
20 ml/4 tsp powdered gelatine
2 eggs, separated
Salt and freshly ground black pepper
Juice of ½ small lemon
175 ml/6 fl oz/¾ cup mayonnaise
4 handfuls of shredded lettuce
10 cm/4 in piece of cucumber, sliced
4 handfuls of watercress
4 artichoke hearts, quartered
60 ml/4 tbsp sunflower seeds
Wedges of lemon, to garnish

1 Drain off the liquor from the fish into a bowl. Add the gelatine and leave to soften for 5 minutes, then stand the bowl in a pan of gently simmering water and stir until dissolved.

2 With the bowl still in the simmering water, beat in the egg yolks and continue to stir until slightly thickened. Remove the bowl from the pan.

3 Remove the skin and bones from the fish and place in a bowl.

4 Beat the yolk mixture into the fish and season to taste with salt, pepper and lemon juice.

5 Whisk the egg whites until they are stiff and form peaks when you remove the whisk.

6 Fold the mayonnaise, then the egg whites into the fish, using a metal spoon. Chill until set.

7 Arrange the salad stuffs on four plates. Spoon the mousse to one side and garnish with wedges of lemon.

Top tip
If eating alone, make up only a quarter of the salad and store the remaining mousse in the fridge for up to 3 days, or freeze and use within 2 months.

Smoked mackerel pâté with cucumber boats

Enjoy this succulent and tasty fish blended with cream cheese, pepper and butter, then packed into chunks of refreshing cucumber. You can also try it with no-carb chicory for a change.

SERVES 4
CARBOHYDRATES: 4 G PER SERVING

❶

2 smoked mackerel fillets, about 150 g/5 oz each
50 g/2 oz/¼ cup butter
50 g/2 oz/¼ cup cream cheese
About 15 ml/1 tbsp lemon juice
Freshly ground black pepper
1 cucumber, cut into quarters

1 Skin the mackerel and purée the flesh in a blender or food processor with the butter and cheese until the mixture is smooth, stopping to scrape down the sides as necessary.

2 Season the pâté with the lemon juice and a little pepper to taste.

3 Halve the cucumber quarters lengthways and scoop out the seeds. Pile the pâté into the cucumber 'boats'.

Top tip
If eating alone, make half the quantity of pâté and store any left over in the fridge, or freeze and use within 2 months.

Cauliflower in baked cheese sauce

This is a delicious alternative to cauliflower in the traditionally carb-laden cheese sauce. It makes a light, nutritious and elegant lunch with plenty of flavour.

SERVES 4

CARBOHYDRATES: 6 G PER SERVING

❶

1 large cauliflower, cut into florets

4 eggs

200 ml/7 fl oz/scant 1 cup crème fraîche

120 ml/4 fl oz/½ cup water

5 ml/1 tsp made English mustard

100 g/4 oz/1 cup grated Cheddar cheese

Salt and freshly ground black pepper

1 Cook the cauliflower in lightly salted boiling water for about 5 minutes or until just tender. Drain thoroughly and tip into an ovenproof dish.

2 Whisk the eggs, then whisk the crème fraîche, water and mustard into them. Stir in half the cheese and season with a very little salt and lots of pepper.

3 Spoon this mixture over the cauliflower and sprinkle with the remaining grated cheese.

4 Bake in a preheated oven at 190°C/375°F/gas 5/fan oven 170°C for about 35 minutes until golden brown on top and the sauce has set.

Grilled goats' cheese salad with walnut oil dressing

Goats' cheese is ideal for grilling as it holds its shape while becoming deliciously soft. It is served on a tender green salad with a walnut oil dressing, which perfectly complements it.

SERVES 4

CARBOHYDRATES: 6 G PER SERVING

❶

4 good handfuls of baby spinach or lettuce leaves

10 cm/4 in piece of cucumber, sliced

4 tomatoes, sliced

4 celery sticks, sliced

60 ml/4 tbsp walnut oil

20 ml/4 tsp balsamic vinegar

Freshly ground black pepper

4 × 70 g/2¾ oz individual rounds of goats' cheese

1 Pile the spinach or lettuce on to four plates. Scatter the cucumber, tomato and celery over.

2 Whisk the walnut oil with the vinegar and a good grinding of pepper. Trickle over the salad.

3 Put the cheeses on a piece of foil on the grill (broiler) rack. Cook under a preheated grill for 2–3 minutes until lightly golden on top but still holding their shape.

4 Transfer to the beds of salad and serve.

Bagna cauda with vegetable dippers

A Mediterranean speciality: anchovies, olive oil, garlic and butter blended to an unctuous dip, served with crisp vegetables. If eating alone, store the rest in the fridge and reheat it.

SERVES 4

CARBOHYDRATES: 6 G PER SERVING

2 heads of chicory (Belgian endive)
2 green (bell) pepper, cut into strips
4 small carrots, cut into short sticks
8 celery sticks, cut into short sticks
For the dip:
2 x 50 g/2 oz/small cans of anchovies
150 ml/¼ pt/⅔ cup olive oil
2 garlic cloves, crushed
50 g/2 oz/¼ cup unsalted (sweet) butter

1 Cut a cone-shaped core out of the base of the heads of chicory, then separate into leaves. Chill all the prepared vegetables until ready to serve.

2 Drain the oil from the anchovies into a saucepan. Add the olive oil and garlic. Chop the fish finely and add it to the pan.

3 Heat, stirring, until gently simmering and the fish 'melts' into the oil. Beat in the butter, a little at a time, until glistening.

4 Pour the mixture into four small bowls and place on plates with the vegetable 'dippers' around. Serve while still hot.

Quiche lorraine with soya and celeriac pastry

The perfect low-carb alternative to ordinary pastry, this has a lovely nutty flavour. You could make a larger quantity and freeze the remainder or store it in the fridge for three days.

SERVES 4

CARBOHYDRATES: 7 G PER SERVING

For the pastry:

100 g/4 oz peeled celeriac (celery root), cut into small chunks

90 g/3½ oz/scant 1 cup full-fat soya flour

45 ml/3 tbsp olive oil

Salt

About 15 ml/1 tbsp cold water

For the filling:

4 rashers (slices) of streaky bacon, rinded and diced

4 spring onions (scallions), chopped

2.5 ml/½ tsp dried mixed herbs

75 g/3 oz/¾ cup grated Cheddar cheese

2 eggs

300 ml/½ pt/1¼ cups fortified unsweetened soya milk

Freshly ground black pepper

1 Boil the celeriac in water for 10 minutes until tender. Drain and mash well.

2 Mix in the flour, oil and a pinch of salt, then add just enough water to form a soft but not sticky dough. Wrap in clingfilm (plastic wrap) and chill for at least 30 minutes.

3 Roll out the pastry (paste) thinly and use to line a 20 cm/8 in flan dish (pie pan) on a baking (cookie) sheet. Prick the base with a fork and line with foil.

4 Bake in a preheated oven at 200°C/400°F/gas 6/fan oven 180°C for 10 minutes. Remove the foil and return to the oven for 5 minutes to dry out.

5 Meanwhile, dry-fry the bacon with the onions in a frying pan (skillet), stirring, until the bacon is almost cooked and the onions have softened.

6 Tip the mixture into the cooked flan case (pie shell) and sprinkle with the herbs and cheese.

7 Beat the eggs with the milk and season with salt and pepper. Pour into the flan. Bake in the oven at 190°C/375°F/gas 5/fan oven 170°C for about 30 minutes until golden and set.

8 Serve warm or cold.

Guacamole with parmesan wafers and chicory

This dip is made with avocado mashed with olive oil and a hint of onion, spiked with lemon juice, Worcestershire and Tabasco sauces, then lightly mixed with tomato and cucumber.

SERVES 4

CARBOHYDRATES: 7 G PER SERVING

For the Parmesan wafers:

100 g/4 oz/1 cup freshly grated Parmesan cheese

For the guacamole:

4 ripe avocados

Juice of ½ lemon

120 ml/4 fl oz/½ cup olive oil, plus extra for greasing

5 ml/1 tsp grated onion

A few drops of Tabasco sauce

A few drops of Worcestershire sauce

Salt and freshly ground black pepper

4 tomatoes, finely chopped

10 cm/4 in piece of cucumber, chopped

4 heads of chicory (Belgian endive)

1 To make the wafers, put 12 spoonfuls of the Parmesan cheese in small piles a little apart on an oiled baking (cookie) sheet and flatten with a fork.

2 Bake in a preheated oven at 200°C/400°F/gas 6/fan oven 180°C for 10 minutes until melted. Remove from the oven and leave to cool and become crisp.

3 To make the guacamole, halve the avocados, remove the stones (pits) and scoop out the flesh into a bowl. Mash well with a fork or balloon whisk.

4 Whisk in the lemon juice, then whisk in the oil a few drops at a time until thick and creamy.

5 Flavour with the onion, Tabasco and Worcestershire sauces and a little salt and pepper. Sharpen with more lemon juice, if liked. Stir in the tomato and cucumber. Spoon into four small pots and put them on individual plates.

6 Cut a cone-shaped core out of the bases of the heads of chicory, then separate into leaves. Arrange around the guacamole and serve with the Parmesan wafers.

Top tip
Once cooled, the Parmesan wafers can be stored for days in an airtight container. They make great nibbles as they have no carbohydrates in them at all.

Crunchy-topped village salad

A fresh salad mingled with the contrasting colours and flavours of black olives and white Feta, topped with toasted pine nuts and bacon and dressed with olive oil, vinegar and oregano.

SERVES 4

CARBOHYDRATES: 8 G PER SERVING

60 ml/4 tbsp pine nuts
100 g/4 oz smoked lardons (diced bacon)
4 good handfuls of shredded white cabbage
4 good handfuls of shredded iceberg lettuce
4 tomatoes, cut into wedges
10cm/4 in piece of cucumber, diced
4 thin slices of onion, separated into rings
24 black olives
175 g/6 oz/1½ cups crumbled Feta cheese
60 ml/4 tbsp olive oil
20 ml/4 tsp red wine vinegar
Freshly ground black pepper
5 ml/1 tsp dried oregano

1 Heat a non-stick frying pan (skillet) and quickly toast the pine nuts until golden. Tip out of the pan and leave to cool.

2 Add the lardons to the pan and stir-fry until crisp and golden, then tip out of the pan and drain on kitchen paper (paper towels).

3 Put the cabbage on a serving plate and arrange the lettuce on top.

4 Scatter the tomato, cucumber, onion and olives over, then top with the crumbled cheese.

5 Trickle the oil and wine vinegar over and season well with pepper. Scatter the pine nuts and lardons over and finish with a sprinkling of oregano.

Avocado with prawns in thousand island dressing

This is a delicious classic: avocado filled with succulent prawns and topped with your favourite pink seafood mayonnaise! It will also make an impressive starter for eight people.

SERVES 4

CARBOHYDRATES: 8 G PER SERVING

❶

4 ripe avocados
Juice of ½ lemon
4 good handfuls of shredded lettuce
10 cm/4 in piece of cucumber, sliced
225 g/8 oz cooked, peeled prawns (shrimp)
60 ml/4 tbsp mayonnaise
20 ml/4 tsp tomato purée (paste)
60 ml/4 tbsp double (heavy) cream
10 ml/2 tsp Worcestershire sauce
Freshly ground black pepper
1.5 ml/¼ tsp cayenne
Wedges of lemon, to garnish

1 Halve the avocados and remove the stones (pits). Brush the cut surfaces with lemon juice.

2 Put the lettuce in four shallow dishes, set the avocado halves on top and arrange the cucumber slices around.

3 Pile the prawns attractively into the cavities in the avocado halves.

4 Mix the mayonnaise with the tomato purée, cream, Worcestershire sauce and a good grinding of pepper. Stir in the cayenne.

5 Spoon the sauce over the prawns and garnish with wedges of lemon.

Starters and Light Snacks

Many of these have no or very few carbohydrates, so are ideal to start a special meal without encroaching on your carb intake for the day. The others are extremely low in carbs, which makes them ideal to team up with one of the lunchtime soups on pages 57, 64 and 65 or with canned consommé.

Chilli-spiced scallops with bacon

If you use frozen scallops, allow them to defrost fully before use. Their sweet, mild flavour and succulent texture marry surprisingly well with chilli and bacon.

SERVES 4
CARBOHYDRATES: 0 G PER SERVING

❶

12 large shelled fresh or frozen scallops
12 rashers (slices) of unsmoked streaky bacon, rinded
60 ml/4 tbsp olive oil
A pinch of chilli powder
Freshly ground black pepper
10 ml/2 tsp lemon juice
Wedges of lemon and a little chopped fresh parsley, to garnish

1 Cut the fresh or defrosted frozen scallops neatly into halves.

2 Stretch each rasher of bacon with the back of a knife, then cut in half lengthways.

3 Roll each piece of scallop in a piece of bacon and secure with a wooden cocktail stick (toothpick), if necessary.

4 Heat the oil in a frying pan (skillet) and fry (sauté) the scallop rolls for 2–3 minutes, turning until cooked through and golden all over.

5 Transfer the scallops to four warm plates and remove the cocktail sticks, if used.

6 Add the chilli powder, a good grinding of pepper and the lemon juice to the oil in the pan and heat, stirring, until sizzling.

7 Pour the oil over the scallops and bacon, then garnish with wedges of lemon and chopped parsley to serve.

Potted prawns with sweet spices

*These are so easy to make and are ideal for entertaining as a
starter or lunch dish as you can prepare them in advance and
chill them, adding the garnish just before serving.*

SERVES 4

CARBOHYDRATES: 0 G PER SERVING

225 g/8 oz/1 cup unsalted (sweet) butter
450 g/1 lb cooked, peeled prawns (shrimp)
1.5 ml/¼ tsp ground mace
A pinch of cayenne
Salt and freshly ground black pepper
Wedges of lemon and sprigs of parsley, to garnish

1 Put half the butter in a saucepan and heat very gently until
melted.

2 Add the prawns and cook gently for 2 minutes until they are
just heated through. Do not allow to boil or the prawns will
become tough.

3 Season to taste with the mace, cayenne, salt and pepper,
then pack into four small ramekins (custard cups).

4 Melt the remaining butter and pour over the tops. Leave to
cool, then chill until firm.

5 Either serve in their pots or turn out on to small plates. Garnish with wedges of lemon and sprigs of parsley to serve.

> **Top tip**
> These are delicious eaten with a crisp breadstick (3 g carb) or a toasted slice of Low-carbohydrate Soya Bread (2 g carb, see page 126) – but not in Phase 1!.

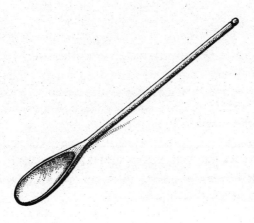

Watercress roulade with cream cheese and chives

Pretty, light and elegant, this cool, green watercress roulade is rolled around a soft cheese and fresh chive filling, then served in thick slices complemented by a nutty sesame dressing.

SERVES 4
CARBOHYDRATES: TRACE PER SERVING

2 bunches of watercress

45 ml/3 tbsp freshly grated Parmesan cheese

Salt and freshly ground black pepper

4 eggs, separated

225 g/8 oz/1 cup cream cheese

30 ml/2 tbsp snipped fresh chives

15 ml/1 tbsp fortified unsweetened soya milk

30 ml/2 tbsp sesame seeds

20 ml/4 tsp sesame oil

30 ml/2 tbsp olive oil

1 Trim the feathery ends off the watercress stalks, then finely chop the leaves, preferably in a blender or food processor. Add 30 ml/2 tbsp of the Parmesan, a little salt and pepper and the egg yolks and beat well.

2 Whisk the egg whites until stiff, then fold in using a metal spoon.

3 Grease and line an 18 × 28 cm/7 × 11 in Swiss roll tin (jelly roll pan) with greased greaseproof (waxed) paper or non-stick baking parchment.

4 Spoon in the watercress mixture and spread out evenly. Bake in a preheated oven at 200°C/400°F/gas 6/fan oven 180°C for 12–15 minutes until risen and firm.

5 Lay another sheet of greaseproof paper or non-stick baking parchment on the work surface and dust with the remaining Parmesan. Turn the roulade out on to the sheet, loosen the cooking paper but leave in place, cover with a clean tea towel (dishcloth) and leave until cold.

6 Beat the cream cheese with the chives and soften slightly with a little soya milk. Season to taste.

7 Toast the sesame seeds in a frying pan (skillet) until golden, then tip out of the pan on to a saucer immediately to prevent burning.

8 Spread the cheese mixture over the cold roulade and roll up. Cut into eight slices and put two slices on each of four small plates.

9 Mix the sesame oil with the olive oil and trickle round the plates. Sprinkle round the plates with a few toasted sesame seeds and serve.

Individual baked eggs with pancetta and chanterelles

The eggs are baked in individual pots over cubes of pancetta and slivers of chanterelles, first fried in olive oil, flavoured with fresh herbs and moistened with cream.

SERVES 4
CARBOHYDRATES: TRACE PER SERVING

❶

50 g/2 oz diced pancetta
50 g/2 oz chanterelles, trimmed and sliced
15 ml/1 tbsp olive oil
8 fresh sage leaves, chopped
4 eggs
Freshly ground black pepper
60 ml/4 tbsp double (heavy) cream
4 small sprigs of fresh sage, to garnish

1 Grease four ramekin dishes (custard cups) with a little olive oil.

2 Fry (sauté) the pancetta and chanterelles in the olive oil for 2 minutes, stirring, until the pancetta is lightly golden but still soft.

3 Spoon the mixture and the juices into the ramekin dishes. Sprinkle with the chopped sage.

4 Break an egg into each pot and season with pepper. Spoon the cream over.

5 Stand the dishes in a baking tin (pan) containing enough boiling water to come half-way up the sides of the dishes. Bake the eggs in a preheated oven at 180°C/350°F/gas 4/fan oven 160°C for 10–15 minutes until cooked to your liking.

6 Place the ramekins on small plates and garnish each plate with a small sprig of fresh sage.

Top tip
Use other well-flavoured mushrooms if chanterelles aren't available. Try other versions, like a handful of prawns in the base, flavoured with a pinch of chilli and cumin, or chopped tomatoes (2 g carb each) and a little grated Cheddar or Mozzarella cheese, flavoured with a few torn basil leaves.

Seafood and wild rocket salad

Prawns, squid, mussels and scallops piled on wild rocket and dressed with mayonnaise, olive oil and fragrant coriander. If you want to serve six, use wine goblets instead of plates.

SERVES 4
CARBOHYDRATES: TRACE PER SERVING

❶

4 good handfuls of wild rocket

1 × 400 g/14 oz packet of frozen cooked seafood cocktail, thawed and drained

For the dressing:

30 ml/2 tbsp mayonnaise

30 ml/2 tbsp olive oil

15 ml/1 tbsp lemon juice

10 ml/2 tsp chopped fresh coriander (cilantro)

Salt and freshly ground black pepper

Sprigs of coriander and wedges of lemon, to garnish

1 Pile the rocket on four individual serving plates.

2 Mix together the dressing ingredients and fold in the seafood cocktail.

3 Spoon on to the rocket and garnish each plate with a sprig of coriander and a wedge of lemon.

Carpaccio of beef with crushed black pepper

Wafer-thin slices of tender fillet steak, coated in crushed black peppercorns, drizzled with olive oil and lemon juice, topped with fresh Parmesan shavings and garnished with wild rocket.

SERVES 4
CARBOHYDRATES: TRACE PER SERVING

❶

350 g/12 oz piece of thick fillet steak
75 ml/5 tbsp olive oil
10 ml/2 tsp crushed black peppercorns
4 handfuls of wild rocket
15 ml/1 tbsp lemon juice
25 g/1 oz/¼ cup freshly shaved Parmesan cheese

1 Trim any sinews from the steak. Brush with 15 ml/1 tbsp of the oil, then roll in the peppercorns to coat thoroughly. Wrap in clingfilm (plastic wrap) and chill for at least 2 hours.

2 Cut the steak into thin slices. Lay the slices side by side, two at a time, between sheets of clingfilm (plastic wrap) and beat with a meat mallet or the end of a rolling pin to flatten until wafer-thin.

3 Arrange the slices overlapping around the edge of four plates. Put a small pile of wild rocket in the centre of each.

4 Trickle the remaining olive oil and the lemon juice over and scatter with the Parmesan shavings.

Melted camembert with blackcurrant and celery

This is a deliciously stylish recipe: warm, melting white cheese wedges served with crisp celery and a drizzle of blackcurrant to offset the richness and complement the flavours.

SERVES 4

CARBOHYDRATES: 1 G PER SERVING

❶

1 whole Camembert, cut into 8 wedges
A little olive oil, for greasing
4 celery sticks, cut into matchsticks
20 ml/4 tsp undiluted sugar-free real blackcurrant cordial

1 Put the Camembert on oiled foil on the grill (broiler) rack. Cook under a preheated grill for 1–2 minutes until beginning to melt.

2 Transfer to warm plates with the celery. Quickly trickle the blackcurrant cordial over the cheese and serve straight away while the cheese is still runny.

Ham, cream cheese and asparagus rolls

Try this simple way with three favourite ingredients – sweet-cured ham, cool, creamy white cheese and asparagus spears – all rolled into one tasty bite. The flavours blend so well.

SERVES 4
CARBOHYDRATES: 1 G PER SERVING

❶

8–12 slices of lean sweet-cured ham (depending on the size)
100 g/4 oz/½ cup cream cheese
Freshly ground black pepper
2 × 300 g/11 oz/medium cans of asparagus spears

1 Lay the ham on a board and spread with the cheese. Season with pepper.

2 Drain the spears and divide between the ham slices, laying them along one edge, then roll up.

Potted stilton with red wine and fennel

A wonderful end to any gourmet meal: ripe Stilton cheese, blended with butter and spices, moistened with red wine and packed into pots, served with cool fennel pieces.

SERVES 4

CARBOHYDRATES: 2 G PER SERVING

175 g/6 oz ripe Stilton
250 g/9 oz/generous 1 cup butter, softened
1.5 ml/¼ tsp ground mace
1.5 ml/¼ tsp paprika
1.5 ml/¼ tsp made English mustard
45 ml/3 tbsp red wine
4 sage leaves
12 juniper berries
2 heads of fennel

1 Discard any rind on the cheese. Mash with half the butter, the spices, mustard and wine until well blended. Pack the mixture into four small pots.

2 Melt the remaining butter. Pour a little over the top of each pot, leaving the sediment behind. Press a sage leaf and three juniper berries into the butter so they are coated. Leave to cool, then chill.

3 Trim the fennel, cut into quarters lengthways and separate into pieces. Put a pot of Stilton on each of four plates and serve with the fennel pieces.

Cheese and sun-dried tomato-stuffed celery

A sensational nibble! The sun-dried tomatoes add flavour and piquancy to this popular savoury with its great combination of soft and crisp textures. It also makes a good alternative to a dessert after a rich dinner.

SERVES 4
CARBOHYDRATES: 2 G PER SERVING ❶

100 g/4 oz/½ cup cream cheese
4 pieces of sun-dried tomato in oil, drained and finely chopped
Freshly ground black pepper
4 large celery sticks

1 Mash the cheese with the tomato, adding freshly ground black pepper to taste.

2 Spread along the celery, then cut into short lengths.

Blue-cheese-stuffed cucumber

A soft, creamy blue cheese like Italian Dolcelatte is ideal for making this cool and appetising snack or savoury but you can use Stilton or Gorgonzola if you prefer.

SERVES 4

CARBOHYDRATES: 2 G PER SERVING

100 g/4 oz/1 cup crumbled soft blue cheese
50 g/2 oz/¼ cup softened butter
A pinch of grated nutmeg
1 small cucumber, quartered

1 Mash the crumbled cheese with the butter and nutmeg until well blended.

2 Halve the cucumber quarters lengthways. Scoop out the seeds with a teaspoon and discard. Dry the cucumber with kitchen paper (paper towels).

3 Pack the cheese into the cucumber and chill until ready to serve.

Lettuce rolls with cheese and cucumber

A clever idea for a cool, tempting, light meal, this dish uses lettuce instead of the traditional bread as a fresh and crisp wrap round a cheese, mayonnaise and cucumber filling.

SERVES 4

CARBOHYDRATES: 3 G PER SERVING

175 g/6 oz/1½ cups grated Cheddar cheese
250 ml/8 fl oz/1 cup mayonnaise
12 large lettuce leaves
1 small cucumber, cut into very thin matchsticks

1 Mix the cheese with the mayonnaise, folding them together thoroughly.

2 Lay the lettuce leaves on a board, undersides up. Spread with the cheese mixture.

3 Lay the cucumber sticks in the centre of one edge of each leaf. Fold in the sides, then roll up so that the shiny upper side of the leaf is on the outside.

Spicy ham and coleslaw rolls

*Another easy-to-make recipe, this involves rolls of tender ham
wrapped round crisp, creamy coleslaw, and lifted with a dash of
spicy Tabasco sauce to give it a bit of extra zing.*

SERVES 4

CARBOHYDRATES: 4 G PER SERVING

8 slices of ham
225 g/8 oz ready-made coleslaw
Tabasco sauce
10 cm/4 in piece of cucumber, sliced

1   Lay the slices of ham on a board. Spoon the coleslaw across
    each slice towards one end.

2   Add a few drops of Tabasco to each pile of coleslaw. Roll up
    and transfer to plates.

3   Serve garnished with the cucumber slices.

Side Dishes and Accompaniments

Whether it's a slice of low-carb bread for toast or some tasty celeriac chips to go with your grilled steak, here you'll find tempting and delicious alternatives to the more usual high-carb accompaniments. There are also some gorgeous low-carb salads to make every meal a gourmet experience! Don't forget to indulge in portions of low-carb vegetables from the list on pages 11–12 too.

Omelette tagliatelle

Serve this no-carb 'tagliatelle' instead of pasta as an accompaniment to any saucy meat, poultry or fish. It goes particularly well with the Turkey, Ham and Cheese Rolls (see page 128).

SERVES 4

CARBOHYDRATES: 0 G PER SERVING

2 large eggs
30 ml/2 tbsp water
Salt and freshly ground black pepper
2.5 ml/½ tsp Italian seasoning
25 g/1 oz/2 tbsp butter
30 ml/2 tbsp olive oil

1 Beat together the eggs and water, then beat in a little salt and pepper and the Italian seasoning.

2 Heat half the butter and olive oil in an omelette pan. Pour in half the egg mixture and cook, lifting the edge to allow the uncooked egg to run underneath. Do not stir, as you would when cooking an omelette – the mixture should remain flat.

3 When golden underneath and almost set, flip the omelette over and cook the other side, then slide out on to a plate and roll up. Cover the plate with foil and keep warm. Repeat with the remaining, butter, oil and egg mixture.

4 Cut the omelette rolls into thin slices, then use as for ordinary tagliatelle.

Rocket and herb salad with sesame seeds

A blend of peppery rocket, fragrant coriander and sweet salad cress, dressed with sesame seeds fried in olive oil until lightly golden. Use extra olive oil if you don't have sesame oil.

SERVES 4

CARBOHYDRATES: TRACE PER SERVING

45 ml/3 tbsp olive oil

15 ml/1 tbsp sesame oil

30 ml/2 tbsp sesame seeds

4 good handfuls of rocket

4 sprigs of fresh coriander (cilantro), torn into small pieces

1 box of salad cress

15 ml/1 tbsp red wine vinegar

Salt and freshly ground black pepper

2.5 ml/½ tsp artificial sweetener

1 Heat the oils in a frying pan (skillet). Add the sesame seeds and fry (sauté) until lightly golden, then remove from the heat immediately and leave to cool.

2 Mix together the rocket, coriander and cress in a salad bowl.

3 Mix the vinegar into the sesame seeds and oil and season to taste with salt, pepper and sweetener. Toss with the salad.

Saffron buns

Delicious and delicately flavoured, these little buns are ideal for breakfast, tea or as a low-carb accompaniment to desserts. Saffron is the most expensive spice and gives a subtle flavour.

MAKES 12
CARBOHYDRATES: 2 G PER BUN

1.5 ml/¼ tsp saffron strands

10 ml/2 tsp boiling water

A little oil, for greasing

4 eggs, separated

90 ml/6 tbsp artificial sweetener, plus extra for dusting

75 g/3 oz/¾ cup full-fat soya flour

20 ml/4 tsp baking powder

50 g/2 oz/¼ cup butter, melted

60 ml/4 tbsp crème fraîche

15 ml/1 tbsp poppy seeds

1 Soak the saffron in the boiling water for 30 minutes to infuse.

2 Grease 12 sections of a tartlet tin (patty pan) or line them with paper cases (cupcake papers).

3 Whisk the egg yolks with the sweetener until thick. Sift the soya flour and baking powder over the surface and fold in with the butter, infused saffron and crème fraîche.

4 Whisk the egg whites until stiff, then fold in with a metal spoon.

5 Spoon the mixture into the prepared tins or paper cases, sprinkle with the poppy seeds and bake in a preheated oven at 180°C/350°F/gas 4/fan oven 160°C for about 8 minutes until firm to the touch, risen and golden. Leave to cool slightly, then remove from the tin and cool on a wire rack.

Low-carbohydrate soya bread

This is a light and tasty bread, the ideal choice for breakfast, lunch or dinner. At only 2 g carbohydrates per slice, you can enjoy it in place of wheat bread with no worries!

MAKES 1 LOAF (10 SLICES)
CARBOHYDRATES: 2 G PER SLICE

50 g/2 oz/½ cup full-fat soya flour
15 ml/1 tbsp baking powder
A good pinch of salt
4 eggs, separated
40 g/1½ oz/3 tbsp butter, melted
45 ml/3 tbsp crème fraîche

1 Sift the soya flour, baking powder and salt together into a bowl.

2 Beat the egg yolks with the butter and crème fraîche until well blended. Beat in the flour mixture.

3 Whisk the egg whites until stiff. Beat 30 ml/2 tbsp into the soya flour mixture, then fold in the remainder with a metal spoon.

4 Turn into a greased 450 g/1 lb loaf tin (pan), base-lined with non-stick baking parchment, and bake in a preheated oven at 180°C/350°F/gas 4/fan oven 160°C for about 40 minutes or until risen, golden and firm to the touch.

5 Turn out on to a wire rack to cool, then store in a polythene bag in the fridge for up to 3 days, or slice and freeze.

Crispy seaweed

Crispy seaweed – which you can buy in supermarkets or from the Chinese take-away – is not seaweed but cabbage. My version makes a delicious accompaniment to any Chinese-style dish.

SERVES 4
CARBOHYDRATES: 2 G PER SERVING   ❶

450 g/1 lb spring (collard) greens, finely shredded
Oil for deep-frying
A few grains of coarse sea salt (optional)

1 Dry the greens really thoroughly on kitchen paper (paper towels).

2 Heat the oil to 190°C/375°F or until a few strands of the greens sizzle and rise to the surface immediately.

3 Deep-fry the shredded greens in batches for 2 minutes until crispy. Drain each batch on kitchen paper (paper towels).

4 Sprinkle with a few grains of coarse sea salt, if liked, before serving.

Fresh green salad with watercress and basil

A simple, fresh crisp salad is the perfect low-carbohydrate accompaniment to almost any meal. You could use rocket or chicory instead of the watercress for a variation.

SERVES 4
CARBOHYDRATES: 2 G PER SERVING

❶

4 good handfuls of torn lettuce leaves
4 good handfuls of watercress, trimmed
10 cm/4 in piece of cucumber, sliced
4 spring onions (scallions), chopped
10 fresh basil leaves, torn
60 ml/4 tbsp olive oil
20 ml/4 tsp red wine vinegar
2.5 ml/½ tsp artificial sweetener
Salt and freshly ground black pepper
5 ml/1 tsp Dijon mustard

1 Put the lettuce, watercress, cucumber and spring onions in a bowl with the basil.

2 Whisk together the remaining ingredients and pour over. Toss gently.

Avocado, bacon and baby spinach salad

Tender young spinach leaves, creamy, cool avocado and crisp diced bacon make a wonderful salad combination here, bathed in a tasty olive oil and cider vinegar dressing.

SERVES 4

CARBOHYDRATES: 2 G PER SERVING

❶

4 rashers (slices) of streaky bacon, rinded and diced
2 avocados, peeled, stoned (pitted) and sliced
4 good handfuls of baby spinach leaves
30 ml/2 tbsp olive oil
10 ml/2 tsp cider vinegar
15 ml/1 tbsp snipped fresh chives
2.5 ml/½ tsp dried mixed herbs
2.5 ml/½ tsp artificial sweetener
Salt and freshly ground black pepper

1 Dry-fry the bacon until crisp and golden. Tip into a bowl. Add the avocado and spinach.

2 Whisk together the remaining ingredients and trickle over. Toss gently.

Celeriac gratin with crème fraîche and garlic

This rich celeriac cake is an elegant low-carb alternative to pommes dauphinoise. If making to serve with Beef in Red Wine (see page 127), put the gratin on a shelf near the top of the oven and cook for slightly longer, if necessary.

SERVES 4

CARBOHYDRATES: 3 G PER SERVING

25 g/1 oz/2 tbsp butter
1 celeriac (celery root), quartered, peeled and sliced
1 garlic clove, crushed
Salt and freshly ground black pepper
100 g/4 oz/1 cup grated Gruyère (Swiss) cheese
2 eggs
150 ml/¼ pt/⅔ cup crème fraîche
150 ml/¼ pt/⅔ cup fortified unsweetened soya milk

1 Grease a large, fairly shallow ovenproof dish with half the butter.

2 Cook the celeriac slices in boiling water for 3–5 minutes until just tender but still holding their shape. Drain well. Layer the celeriac in the dish with the cheese, sprinkling with the garlic and some salt and pepper as you go, and finishing with a layer of cheese.

3 Beat the eggs with the crème fraîche and milk. Pour over the celeriac.

4 Bake in a preheated oven at 180°C/350°F/gas 4/fan oven 160°C for about 45 minutes until set and lightly golden.

Thick golden celeriac chips

These are an ingenious alternative to French fries – something low-carb dieters often miss! They taste superb and, of course, they are incredibly low in carbohydrates.

SERVES 4

CARBOHYDRATES: 3 G PER SERVING

1 celeriac (celery root), peeled and cut into thick fingers
Oil for shallow-frying

1 Cook the celeriac in boiling water for 2 minutes. Drain thoroughly.

2 Heat about 2 cm/³/₄ in of oil in a frying pan (skillet). Add half the celeriac and cook for about 3 minutes, turning occasionally, until golden brown.

3 Remove from the pan, drain on kitchen paper (paper towels) and keep warm in a low oven while repeating with the remaining celeriac.

4 Serve hot.

Broccoli and cauliflower sauté with coriander seeds

A perfect accompaniment to beef, this dish is made up of tiny florets of broccoli and cauliflower tossed in olive oil with fragrant coriander seeds and flavoured with just a hint of garlic.

SERVES 4

CARBOHYDRATES: 3 G PER SERVING

30 ml/2 tbsp olive oil
1 small cauliflower, cut into tiny florets
225 g/8 oz broccoli, cut into tiny florets
10 ml/2 tsp coriander (cilantro) seeds, crushed
1 garlic clove, crushed
Salt and freshly ground black pepper

1 Heat the oil in a frying pan (skillet). Add the cauliflower and broccoli and fry (sauté) for 2 minutes, stirring.

2 Add the coriander, garlic, a very little salt and lots of pepper. Cook, stirring, for about 5 minutes until just tender and slightly golden round the edges.

Greek-style mixed salad with feta cheese

This simple and deliciously fresh salad can be served on its own as a light lunch, with a crunchy low-carb roll to make a more filling meal, or as a side dish, especially with grilled meats.

SERVES 4

CARBOHYDRATES: 4 G PER SERVING   ❶

4 good handfuls of shredded lettuce

10 cm/4 in piece of cucumber, diced

4 tomatoes, diced

1 spring onion (scallion), finely chopped

100 g/4 oz/1 cup diced Feta cheese

50 g/2 oz/⅓ cup black olives

2.5 ml/½ tsp dried oregano

30 ml/2 tbsp olive oil

10 ml/2 tsp red wine vinegar

Salt and freshly ground black pepper

1 Arrange the lettuce on four small plates. Scatter the cucumber, tomato and spring onion over.

2 Sprinkle the cheese, olives and oregano on top of the other ingredients.

3 Drizzle with the oil and vinegar and season lightly.

Beetroot crisps

These are not only a delicious accompaniment to any main course – especially grilled steaks – but they also make a sumptuous nibble with pre-dinner drinks.

SERVES 4

CARBOHYDRATES: 7 G PER SERVING

4 raw beetroot (red beets)
Oil, for deep-frying
A little coarse sea salt (optional)

1 Peel the beetroot and cut into very thin slices with a mandolin slicer or a very sharp knife. Dry on kitchen paper (paper towels).

2 Deep-fry the slices in hot oil for about 2½ minutes until crisp and turning orange-pink. Don't cook any longer or they will burn. Drain on kitchen paper.

3 Sprinkle with coarse sea salt, if liked, before serving.

Creamy celeriac and carrot mash

*A wonderful alternative to potato mash – whether or not
potatoes are forbidden! A delicious dish, it is high in fibre and
sumptuous in flavour and will be enjoyed by all the family.*

SERVES 4

CARBOHYDRATES: 9 G PER SERVING

1 small celeriac (celery root), cut into small chunks

4 carrots, sliced

A good knob of butter

30 ml/2 tbsp double (heavy) cream

Freshly ground black pepper

1 Boil the celeriac and carrot together in lightly salted water
for about 8–10 minutes until tender. Drain well.

2 Mash thoroughly with the butter and cream, then beat in a
good grinding of pepper.

Tuscan roasted vegetables

*These colourful Mediterranean vegetables are gorgeous served
with plain grilled chops, chicken or fresh tuna steaks.
Alternatively, serve them for lunch topped with fried or
poached eggs.*

SERVES 4

CARBOHYDRATES: 9 G PER SERVING   ❶

1 red (bell) pepper, cut into wide strips
1 green pepper, cut into wide strips
2 courgettes (zucchini), diagonally sliced
1 aubergine (eggplant), sliced
5 ml/1 tsp dried rosemary, crushed
90 ml/6 tbsp olive oil
Freshly ground black pepper

1 Preheat the oven to 180°C/350°F/gas 4/fan oven 160°C.
Put all the prepared vegetables in a roasting tin (pan) and
sprinkle with the rosemary and the olive oil.

2 Season with lots of pepper and toss with your hands so that
all the vegetables are coated in the oil, then spread out in an
even layer.

3 Bake towards the top of the oven for about 45 minutes until
tender and well-browned round the edge.

Main Meals

All these delicious recipes are elegant enough to serve to guests but are also simply fabulous any day of the week as they're all so easy to make. If you're eating alone, most quantities can easily be quartered but, if you're making a casserole, you may as well make the whole thing, then either eat it over the next few days or freeze it in individual portions.

Lamb shanks with rosemary jus

Meltingly tender garlic-flavoured lamb lifted with rosemary and blackcurrant. They are lovely served on a bed of Creamy Celeriac and Carrot Mash (see page 111) and a fresh green salad.

SERVES 4
CARBOHYDRATES: TRACE PER SERVING

4 lamb shanks
1 garlic clove, cut into slivers
4 large sprigs of fresh rosemary, plus small sprigs for garnishing
600 ml/1 pt/2½ cups lamb or chicken stock, made with
1 stock cube
45 ml/3 tbsp undiluted sugar-free real blackcurrant cordial
Salt and freshly ground black pepper

1 Make a few small cuts in the lamb with a sharp-pointed knife and insert a sliver of garlic into each.

2 Put the large sprigs of rosemary in a small casserole dish (Dutch oven) and lay the lamb on top.

3 Pour the stock around and add the cordial. Sprinkle the meat with salt and pepper. Cover with the lid or foil.

4 Cook in a preheated oven at 160°C/325°F/gas 3/fan oven 145°C for 2½–3 hours until meltingly tender.

5 Lift the lamb out of the casserole and keep warm. Discard the rosemary.

6 Spoon off any fat floating on the surface. Boil the juices rapidly until reduced and syrupy. Taste and re-season, if necessary.

7 Transfer the lamb to warm serving plates and spoon the juices over. Garnish each serving with a small sprig of rosemary.

Steak with grainy mustard jus

Thick, juicy sirloin steaks bathed in a white wine, brandy and crème fraîche sauce flavoured with mustard. Try it with Beetroot Crisps (see page 110) and French beans (5 g carb per serving).

SERVES 4
CARBOHYDRATES: 1 G PER SERVING

4 sirloin steaks, about 175 g/6 oz each
Salt and freshly ground black pepper
15 g/½ oz/1 tbsp butter
15 ml/1 tbsp olive oil
120 ml/4 fl oz/½ cup dry white wine
15 ml/1 tbsp wholegrain mustard
15 ml/1 tbsp brandy
120 ml/4 fl oz/½ cup crème fraîche
1.5 ml/¼ tsp artificial sweetener
Chopped fresh parsley, to garnish

1 Wipe the steaks and season with salt and pepper. Fry (sauté) in the butter and oil for 2 minutes on each side to brown, then turn down the heat and cook for a further 2–10 minutes, turning once, until cooked to your liking. Remove from the pan and keep warm.

2 Add the wine to the pan and boil until reduced by half. Stir in the mustard, brandy, crème fraîche and sweetener and season to taste. Remove from the heat.

3   Transfer the steaks to warm plates and spoon the sauce over. Garnish with chopped parsley.

Grilled cheese-topped gammon

A nutty-sweet, melting cheese is the ideal topping for juicy tender gammon steaks and is perfect with young French beans (5 g carb per serving) and sautéed courgettes.

SERVES 4
CARBOHYDRATES: 2 G PER SERVING   ❶

1 large leek, thinly sliced
A good knob of butter or margarine
15 ml/1 tbsp olive oil
4 gammon steaks
Freshly ground black pepper
8 slices of Havarti or Emmental (Swiss) cheese

1   Put the leek in a saucepan with the butter or margarine and oil. Cook over a fairly gentle heat, stirring all the time, for about 4 minutes until soft.

2   Snip all round the edge of the gammon steaks with scissors to stop it curling when cooked. Place on the grill (broiler) rack, add a grinding of pepper and cook for about 3 minutes on each side until golden and cooked through.

3   Spread the leek on top of each gammon steak. Lay the slices of cheese on top and return to the grill until melted.

117

Grilled mackerel with mustard rub

*The mustard rub brings out all the flavour and succulence
of fresh mackerel, and the fresh runner beans offset the
richness. Serve with baby carrots (5 g carb per serving).*

SERVES 4

CARBOHYDRATES: 2 G PER SERVING

❶

5 ml/1 tsp mustard powder

5 ml/1 tsp dried oregano

5 ml/1 tsp paprika

5 ml/1 tsp onion salt

2.5 ml/½ tsp artificial sweetener

Salt and freshly ground black pepper

4 large mackerel, cleaned

450 g/1 lb runner beans, trimmed and diagonally sliced

A little oil for greasing

1 Mix the mustard powder with the oregano, paprika, onion salt, sweetener and a good grinding of pepper.

2 Rinse the mackerel and dry with kitchen paper (paper towels). Cut off the heads, if preferred.

3 Make several slashes in the bodies on both sides and rub the mustard mixture into these slits. Chill for at least 2 hours to allow the flavours to develop.

4 When ready to cook, bring a pan of water with a pinch of salt to the boil and preheat the grill (broiler). Oil the rack, then put the mackerel on it and grill (broil) for 4–5 minutes until golden. Turn over and cook the other side for 4–5 minutes until golden brown and cooked through.

5 At the same time, put the beans in the pan of boiling water and boil for about 4 minutes until just tender but still with some bite. Drain well.

6 Spoon the beans on to four warm plates and spread out to form beds. Lay the mackerel on top of the beans and serve hot.

Top tip
Try this recipe with herring or red mullet too.

Tandoori chicken with cucumber raita

Rich, red, mildly spiced marinated chicken baked until tinged black on the outside but juicy and succulent inside. Serve it with popadoms (6 g carb each) and a fresh green salad (see page 104).

SERVES 4

CARBOHYDRATES: 3 G PER SERVING

For the tandoori chicken:

2 small chickens, each 1.25 kg/2½ lb, or 4 large chicken portions

Juice of 1 lime or small lemon

2.5 ml/½ tsp each of red and yellow food colouring

300 ml/½ pt/1¼ cups plain strained Greek-style cow's milk yoghurt

1 small garlic clove, crushed

2.5 ml/½ tsp ground ginger

15 ml/1 tbsp garam masala

15 ml/1 tbsp paprika

1.5 ml/¼ tsp chilli powder

For the raita:

½ cucumber, finely diced

10 ml/2 tsp dried mint

150 ml/¼ pt/⅔ cup plain strained Greek-style cow's milk yoghurt

Salt and freshly ground black pepper
Wedges of lemon and sprigs of fresh coriander (cilantro),
to serve

1 To make the tandoori chicken, pull off and discard as much of the skin from the chicken as possible. Cut each bird into quarters and make several slashes in the flesh.

2 Mix the lime or lemon juice with the food colourings and brush all over the chicken.

3 Mix the yoghurt with the garlic and spices in a large roasting tin (pan). Turn the chicken pieces in the mixture to coat completely, rubbing it well into the slits. Cover and leave to marinate for at least 3 hours, turning at least once.

4 Arrange the chicken pieces flesh-sides down and transfer the roasting tin to a preheated oven at 200°C/400°F/gas 6/fan oven 180°C. Cook for 20 minutes, then drain off most of the liquid. Turn the chicken over and cook for a further 20 minutes.

5 Meanwhile, to make the raita, mix the cucumber with the mint and yoghurt and season to taste. Turn into a small bowl and chill until ready to serve.

6 Transfer the chicken to warm plates. Garnish with wedges of lemon and sprigs of coriander and serve with the raita.

Pan-roasted chicken with mushrooms and turnips

Sautéed chicken, mushrooms and turnips, subtly flavoured with garlic and fresh parsley, then served with all the rich, buttery pan juices poured over the top. Serve it with a fresh green salad (see page 104).

SERVES 4

CARBOHYDRATES: 3 G PER SERVING

❶

50 g/2 oz/¼ cup butter
60 ml/4 tbsp olive oil
4 chicken leg portions
450 g/1 lb turnips, cut into walnut-sized pieces
225 g/8 oz button mushrooms
Salt and freshly ground black pepper
45 ml/3 tbsp chopped fresh parsley
2 garlic cloves, chopped
300 ml/½ pt/1¼ cups chicken stock, made with 1 stock cube

1 Heat half the butter and half the oil in a large frying pan (skillet) or wok. Add the chicken and fry (sauté) for about 5 minutes until browned all over. Remove from the pan.

2 Add the remaining butter and oil and fry the turnips for 2–3 minutes, stirring and turning until lightly golden.

3 Return the chicken to the pan and add the mushrooms. Season lightly with salt and pepper. Turn down the heat, cover the pan with a lid or foil and cook gently for about 30 minutes until the chicken and turnips are tender.

4 Sprinkle the parsley and garlic over, re-cover and cook for a further 5 minutes.

5 Remove the chicken and vegetables from the pan and keep warm.

6 Pour the stock into the pan and boil, stirring, until slightly reduced. Spoon over the chicken and serve.

Warm smoked haddock and quails' egg salad

A sensational salad of golden smoked haddock, tiny quails' eggs and crisp Italian bacon on a bed of baby spinach, bathed in a warm dressing of olive oil, crème fraîche and red wine vinegar.

SERVES 4

CARBOHYDRATES: 4 G PER SERVING

4 pieces of smoked haddock fillet, about 175 g/6 oz each

12 quails' eggs, scrubbed

225 g/8 oz diced pancetta

8 good handfuls of baby spinach leaves

8 cherry tomatoes, quartered

10 cm/4 in piece of cucumber, diced

30 ml/2 tbsp snipped fresh chives

120 ml/4 fl oz/½ cup olive oil

45 ml/3 tbsp red wine vinegar

45 ml/3 tbsp crème fraîche

2.5 ml/½ tsp artificial sweetener

Salt and freshly ground black pepper

1 Put the fish in a shallow pan and cover with water. Put the quails' eggs alongside. Bring to the boil, boil for just 30 seconds for soft-boiled (soft-cooked) eggs or exactly 3 minutes for hard-boiled (hard-cooked), then quickly remove the eggs and put them in a bowl of cold water to prevent further cooking.

2 Cover the pan and poach the fish for a further 5 minutes or until tender. Drain. Remove the skin and cut the fish into bite-sized pieces.

3 Dry-fry the pancetta in a frying pan (skillet), stirring until crisp. Remove from the pan with a draining spoon and drain on kitchen paper (paper towels).

4 Pile the spinach on to four plates and scatter the pancetta, fish, tomatoes, cucumber and chives over.

5 Shell and halve the eggs and arrange around, taking care if they are soft-boiled as the yolks will be runny.

6 Put the oil and wine vinegar in the pan with the pancetta fat and bring to the boil, stirring. Stir in the crème fraîche and season with sweetener, salt and lots of pepper. Spoon over the salad and serve straight away.

Chicken and bamboo shoots with pak choi

An exciting stir-fry of tender strips of chicken, mushrooms, spring onions, bamboo shoots and shredded green pak choi, tossed in soy sauce and lightly flavoured with Chinese spices.

SERVES 4
CARBOHYDRATES: 4 G PER SERVING   ❶

45 ml/3 tbsp sunflower oil

4 skinless chicken breasts, cut into thin strips

1 bunch of spring onions (scallions), diagonally sliced into
5 cm/2 in lengths

1 × 225 g/8 oz/small can of bamboo shoots, drained

4 heads of pak choi, shredded

225 g/8 oz oyster mushrooms, sliced

20 ml/4 tsp soy sauce

15 ml/1 tbsp water

2.5 ml/½ tsp Chinese five-spice powder

1 Heat the oil in a frying pan (skillet) or wok. Add the chicken and stir-fry for 3 minutes. Add the spring onions and stir-fry for 2 minutes. Add the bamboo shoots, pak choi and mushrooms and stir-fry for 4 minutes until everything is just cooked.

2 Stir in the soy sauce, water and five-spice powder and toss well before serving.

Beef in red wine

*Steak slowly cooked in red wine with lardons, herbs, garlic and
vegetables until meltingly tender. Serve with Celeriac Gratin
(see page 106) and mangetout (2 g carb per serving).*

SERVES 4
CARBOHYDRATES: 5 G PER SERVING

700 g/1½ lb braising steak, diced
50 g/2 oz lardons (diced bacon)
1 red onion, chopped
1 garlic clove, crushed
1 large carrot, sliced
225 g/8 oz baby button mushrooms
300 ml/½ pt/1¼ cups red wine
150 ml/¼ pt/⅔ cup beef stock made with ½ a stock cube
15 ml/1 tbsp tomato purée (paste)
Salt and freshly ground black pepper
30 ml/2 tbsp snipped fresh chives

1 Put all the ingredients except the chives in a flameproof
casserole dish (Dutch oven) and bring to the boil.

2 Cover with a lid and transfer to a preheated oven at
160°C/325°F/gas 3/fan oven 140°C for 2½ hours.

3 Stir the casserole, taste and re-season if necessary. Sprinkle
with the chives and serve hot.

Turkey, ham and cheese rolls with tomato coulis

Thin turkey steaks, rolled round sweet-cured ham and cheese, sautéed, then sliced and served with a rich tomato sauce. Serve with Omelette Tagliatelle (see page 98) and mangetout (2 g carb per serving).

SERVES 4
CARBOHYDRATE: 5 G PER SERVING ❶

4 turkey breast steaks, about 175 g/6 oz each
4 slices of sweet-cured cooked ham
4 slices of Leerdammer or Emmental (Swiss) cheese
For the coulis:
1 red onion, finely chopped
30 ml/2 tbsp olive oil
1 garlic clove, crushed
1 × 400 g/14 oz/large can of chopped tomatoes
15 ml/1 tbsp tomato purée (paste)
Salt and freshly ground black pepper
1.5 ml/¼ tsp artificial sweetener
15 ml/1 tbsp chopped fresh basil
Oil for shallow-frying
Sprigs of basil, to garnish

1 Put the steaks one at a time in a plastic bag and beat with a rolling pin or meat mallet to flatten.

2 Lay a slice of ham and a slice of cheese on each steak and roll up. Secure each with a wooden cocktail stick (toothpick).

3 To make the coulis, in a saucepan fry (sauté) the onion in the olive oil for 2 minutes, stirring. Add the garlic, tomatoes and tomato purée. Bring to the boil, stirring, then reduce the heat and simmer for about 5 minutes, stirring occasionally until thick. Season to taste and stir in the sweetener and basil. Remove from the heat.

4 Heat a little oil in a frying pan (skillet). Add the turkey rolls and fry, turning occasionally, for 8 minutes until cooked through and golden. Reheat the coulis.

5 Remove the cocktail sticks from the turkey and cut each roll into six slices. Lay on individual plates, spoon a little coulis over, garnish with sprigs of basil and serve straight away.

Greek-style aubergine moussaka

This is a perfect recipe to serve when you are entertaining guests because not only can it be made in advance but also no one will guess it's low-carb! Serve with a Greek-style Mixed Salad (see page 109).

SERVES 4

CARBOHYDRATES: 8 G PER SERVING   ❶

90 ml/6 tbsp olive oil

2 small aubergines (eggplant), sliced

1 onion, chopped

450 g/1 lb minced (ground) lamb

20 ml/4 tsp tomato purée (paste)

250 ml/8 fl oz/1 cup water

2.5 ml/½ tsp ground cinnamon

2.5 ml/½ tsp dried oregano

Salt and freshly ground black pepper

2 eggs, beaten

250 ml/8 fl oz/1 cup crème fraîche

50 g/2 oz/½ cup grated Cheddar cheese

1 Heat 60 ml/4 tbsp of the oil in a frying pan (skillet). Fry (sauté) the aubergine slices until golden on both sides. Drain on kitchen paper (paper towels).

2 Heat the remaining oil in a saucepan. Add the onion and lamb and cook, stirring, until the lamb is no longer pink and all the grains are separate.

3 Stir in the tomato purée, water, cinnamon and oregano and season to taste with salt and pepper. Simmer, stirring occasionally, for 5 minutes.

4 Layer the meat and aubergine slices in an ovenproof dish, finishing with a layer of aubergine.

5 Whisk the eggs and crème fraîche together with a good grinding of pepper. Stir in the cheese and spoon over the aubergine layer.

6 Bake in a preheated oven at 190°C/375°F/gas 5/fan oven 170°C for about 40 minutes until the top is golden and set.

7 Serve the moussaka hot or at room temperature.

Beef stroganoff with mushrooms and brandy

Strips of tender fillet steak, quickly cooked with mushrooms and onion, bathed in a crème fraîche sauce laced with brandy. Try serving this with Broccoli and Cauliflower Sauté (see page 108).

SERVES 4
CARBOHYDRATES: 8 G PER SERVING ❶

3 onions, sliced
225 g/8 oz button mushrooms, sliced
25 g/1 oz/2 tbsp butter
450 g/1 lb fillet steak, cut into thin strips
Salt and freshly ground black pepper
45 ml/3 tbsp brandy
300 ml/½ pt/1¼ cups crème fraîche
30 ml/2 tbsp chopped fresh parsley

1 Fry (sauté) the onions and mushrooms in the butter for 3 minutes, stirring, until softened but only lightly golden.

2 Add the steak and continue to stir-fry for 3–4 minutes until the steak is just cooked.

3 Season well, then pour over the brandy and ignite. Shake the pan until the flames subside, then stir in the crème fraîche and parsley. Simmer for about 2 minutes until slightly thickened. Taste and re-season, if necessary.

Chicken and vegetable stir-fry

Tender chicken breast strips stir-fried with a selection of vegetables, flavoured in oriental style. You could serve this with some Omelette Tagliatelle (see page 98).

SERVES 4
CARBOHYDRATES: 10 G PER SERVING

4 skinless chicken breasts, cut into strips
30 ml/2 tbsp sunflower oil
1 bunch of spring onions (scallions), cut into short lengths
1 large carrot, cut into matchsticks
½ cucumber, cut into matchsticks
1 green and 1 red (bell) pepper, sliced
1 garlic clove, crushed
1 × 225 g/8 oz/small can of bamboo shoots, drained
100 g/4 oz/2 cups beansprouts
30 ml/2 tbsp soy sauce
30 ml/2 tbsp dry sherry
2.5 ml/½ tsp ground ginger
2.5 ml/½ tsp artificial sweetener

1 Stir-fry the chicken in the oil for 3 minutes.

2 Add all the vegetables and stir-fry for 3 minutes.

3 Add all the remaining ingredients and cook for 2 minutes.

Thai prawn and cucumber curry with wild rice

Subtle flavours of lemon grass and coconut with garlic, spring onions and a selection of sweet and hot spices are blended together in this creamy curry, packed with king prawns.

SERVES 4
CARBOHYDRATES: 10 G PER SERVING

225 g/8 oz/1 cup wild rice
1 cucumber, quartered lengthways and cut into
bite-sized chunks
15 g/¹/₂ oz/1 tbsp butter
2 garlic cloves, crushed
5 ml/1 tsp grated fresh root ginger
1 stalk of lemon grass, finely chopped
1 bunch of spring onions (scallions), finely chopped
5 ml/1 tsp ground turmeric
10 ml/2 tsp garam masala
1.5 ml/¹/₄ tsp ground cloves
2.5 ml/¹/₂ tsp ground cinnamon
2 green chillies, seeded and finely chopped
5 ml/1 tsp artificial sweetener
100 g/4 oz/¹/₂ block of creamed coconut, cut into chunks
450 ml/³/₄ pt/2 cups fish stock, made with 1 stock cube

400 g/14 oz raw peeled king prawns (jumbo shrimp), split in
half lengthways
Salt and freshly ground black pepper
A few fresh chive stalks, to garnish

1 Cook the wild rice in lightly salted boiling water for 20–30
minutes until just tender but still with some 'bite'. Drain.

2 Meanwhile, put the cucumber in a pan with just enough
water to cover. Add a pinch of salt. Bring to the boil, reduce
the heat and simmer for 5 minutes. Drain.

3 Melt the butter in a saucepan. Add the garlic, ginger, lemon
grass, spring onions, all the spices and the chillies. Cook,
stirring, for 1 minute.

4 Add the sweetener, coconut and stock. Bring to the boil and
simmer, stirring all the time, until the coconut melts.

5 Add the prawns and cucumber and simmer for 5 minutes,
stirring. Season to taste.

6 Pile the wild rice into warm bowls and spoon the curry
over. Garnish each with a few chive stalks and serve.

Top tip
You must use pure wild rice, not wild rice mix, which has
long-grain rice added.

Grilled tuna with peppers and olives

Tuna is a meaty, tasty fish. Here it's flavoured with the subtle, smoky flavour of Spanish pimentón, cooked until just pink and served with colourful grilled peppers and stuffed olives.

SERVES 4

CARBOHYDRATES: 10 G PER SERVING ❶

4 tuna steaks, about 175 g/6 oz each
90 ml/6 tbsp olive oil
10 ml/2 tsp sweet pimentón
Salt and freshly ground black pepper
4 green (bell) peppers, cut into thick strips
2 yellow peppers, cut into thick strips
1 red pepper, cut into thick strips
15 ml/1 tbsp chopped fresh parsley
16 stuffed olives, sliced

1 Brush the tuna with a little of the oil and season on both sides with the pimentón, a very little salt and lots of black pepper.

2 Toss the pepper strips in the remaining oil and arrange on foil in the grill (broiler) pan. Cook under a preheated grill for 5 minutes, then turn over and grill (broil) for a further 5 minutes.

3 Put the grill rack on top of the peppers and arrange the tuna steaks on it. Grill for 2 minutes. Turn the tuna over and rearrange the pepper slices so that they can brown evenly round the sides of the tuna. Grill for a further 2–4 minutes until the fish is just cooked but slightly pink in the centre and the peppers are browning at the edges.

4 Carefully lift the grill rack off the peppers. Transfer the peppers to warm plates with any juices. Top with the tuna. Sprinkle the tuna with the parsley and scatter the olives around.

Top tip
Try this delicious dish with some sautéed courgettes (zucchini) (3 g carb per serving) and some wilted (lightly cooked) spinach (1 g carb per serving).

Desserts

Many desserts are packed with sugar so are full of carbohydrates, but these are all carefully designed to give you maximum flavour and sumptuousness without piling on the carbs. There's no more than 5 g carb per serving in even the most decadent of them!

Blackcurrant fluff

Try experimenting with other flavoured cordials instead of the blackcurrant. There are plenty of exotic flavours to choose from – but do check their carbohydrate content before using them.

SERVES 4
CARBOHYDRATES: TRACE PER SERVING

4 eggs
60 ml/4 tbsp undiluted sugar-free real blackcurrant cordial

1 Break the eggs into a bowl and whisk in the cordial until well blended.

2 Put the bowl over a pan of gently simmering water and whisk continuously until thick and fluffy.

3 Spoon into four glasses and serve.

Zabaglione

This traditional Italian dessert can take some time to whisk but don't give up too soon otherwise it will collapse before you eat it. Try serving it with a Saffron Bun (see page 100).

SERVES 4
CARBOHYDRATES: TRACE PER SERVING

2 eggs
30 ml/2 tbsp artificial sweetener
45 ml/3 tbsp dry sherry

1 Break the eggs into a bowl. Whisk in the sweetener and the dry sherry.

2 Stand the bowl over a pan of gently simmering water and whisk, preferably with an electric beater, for 10–20 minutes until thick and fluffy.

3 Spoon into four wine glasses and serve straight away.

Grilled avocado slices with crème fraîche

This is a stylish and elegant dessert: slices of creamy-smooth avocado brushed with butter and flavoured with lime or lemon, then lightly grilled, sweetened and served with crème fraîche.

SERVES 4

CARBOHYDRATES: 1 G PER SERVING   ❶

2 small ripe avocados
50 g/2 oz/¼ cup butter
Finely grated zest of 1 lime or 1 small lemon
Artificial sweetener (optional)
60 ml/4 tbsp crème fraîche

1   Peel, halve, stone (pit) and slice the avocados. Place on a grill (broiler) rack.

2   Melt the butter with the lime or lemon zest and brush all over the avocado slices. Grill (broil) for about 3 minutes until turning lightly golden.

3   Transfer the slices to warm plates and sprinkle with a little artificial sweetener, if liked.

4   Serve with a spoonful of crème fraîche.

Creamy chocolate custard dessert

This velvety pudding is similar to the commercial chocolate desserts you can buy in the chiller cabinet at your favourite supermarket – but has far fewer carbohydrates.

SERVES 4
CARBOHYDRATES: 1 G PER SERVING

20 ml/4 tsp cocoa (unsweetened chocolate) powder
350 ml/12 fl oz/1⅓ cups boiling water
120 ml/4 fl oz/½ cup double (heavy) cream
2 large eggs
60 ml/4 tbsp artificial sweetener

1 Blend the cocoa with the boiling water in a small heavy-based saucepan.

2 Add the cream and whisk in the eggs. Cook over a gentle heat, stirring all the time with a wooden spoon, until thickened. Do not allow to boil. Add the sweetener.

3 Spoon into four wine goblets and cover with clingfilm (plastic wrap) to prevent a skin forming. Leave to cool, then chill until ready to serve.

Fresh lemon and lime sorbet

A cool, refreshing dessert that's perfect for rounding off any meal. You can make double or triple the quantity if you find you like it – I always have a large tubful in the freezer.

SERVES 6

CARBOHYDRATES: 1 G PER SERVING

15 ml/1 tbsp powdered gelatine
175 ml/6 fl oz/¾ cup water
Finely grated zest and juice of 1 lime
Finely grated zest of 1 lemon
Juice of 4 lemons
Artificial sweetener, to taste
1 egg white

1 Mix the gelatine with 45 ml/3 tbsp of the water and leave to soften for 5 minutes. Either stand the bowl in a pan of hot water and stir until completely dissolved or heat briefly in the microwave – but do not allow to boil.

2 Stir in the remaining water, the lime and lemon zests and the juices.

3 Sweeten to taste with artificial sweetener – it should taste very sweet but still 'tangy'.

4 Pour the mixture into a freezer-proof container, cover and freeze for 2 hours or until firm around the edges.

5 Whisk thoroughly with a fork to break up the ice crystals. Whisk the egg white until stiff, then fold into the lemon and lime mixture with a metal spoon.

6 Re-cover and freeze for a further 1½ hours, then whisk thoroughly with a fork again. Cover and freeze until firm.

7 About 15 minutes before serving, transfer the sorbet to the fridge to soften slightly. Pop any left back in the freezer as soon as possible.

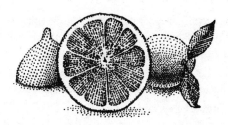

Mediterranean-style coffee granita

A cool and refreshing way to round off a delicious meal. You can make as much of this as you like, but if you leave it until really hard you'll have to crush it in a blender or food processor!

SERVES 4

CARBOHYDRATES: 1 G PER SERVING ❶

600 ml/1 pt/2½ cups boiling water
45 ml/3 tbsp instant coffee granules
60 ml/4 tbsp artificial sweetener

1 Mix the water with the coffee until dissolved, then add the artificial sweetener – it should taste very sweet.

2 Pour the mixture into a freezer-proof container and leave to cool.

3 Transfer to the freezer for about 1 hour until frozen around the edges. Whisk well with a fork to break up the ice crystals, then return to the freezer.

4 Repeat the freezing and whisking twice more – it should take about 3 hours in all – until granular.

5 Spoon into glasses and serve.

Rhubarb fool with fresh ginger

This is the perfect fruit fool – rich and creamy but with just a hint of spice. Try using 450 g/1 lb gooseberries instead of the rhubarb and omit the ginger if you prefer.

SERVES 4

CARBOHYDRATES: 2 G PER SERVING

❶

4 sticks of rhubarb, cut into short lengths
5 ml/1 tsp grated fresh root ginger
Artificial sweetener, to taste
175 ml/6 fl oz/³⁄₄ cup double (heavy) cream

1 Put the rhubarb in a pan. Heat very gently until the juice runs, then cover the pan and cook over a gentle heat, stirring occasionally, until really soft.

2 If there is still quite a lot of juice, boil rapidly to evaporate it, stirring all the time. Stir in the ginger and sweetener to taste. Remove from the heat and leave until cold.

3 Whip the cream until stiff. Fold in the cold rhubarb until just blended, then spoon into four glasses and chill until ready to serve.

Rum and chocolate mousse

Chocolate and rum blend beautifully in this rich and delicious mousse. If you are eating alone, make half the quantity and either chill the rest for another day or share it with a friend.

SERVES 4
CARBOHYDRATES: 2 G PER SERVING

❶

20 ml/4 tsp cocoa (unsweetened chocolate) powder
30 ml/2 tbsp boiling water
30 ml/2 tbsp artificial sweetener
2.5 ml/½ tsp rum essence (extract)
2 eggs, separated
120 ml/4 fl oz/½ cup double (heavy) cream

1 Blend the cocoa with the boiling water and sweetener and stir until smooth. Stir in the rum essence and whisk in the egg yolks.

2 Whisk the egg whites until stiff. Whisk the cream separately until peaking. Fold the cream into the cocoa mixture, then finally fold in the egg white. Taste and add more rum essence, if liked.

3 Turn into small serving dishes and chill until firm.

Almond-flavoured jelly cream

*Try serving this cool, smooth jelly with some fresh raspberries
(an added 5 g carbs per portion) to make an even more
tempting dessert.*

SERVES 4

CARBOHYDRATES: 2 G PER SERVING

❶

15 ml/1 tbsp powdered gelatine
350 ml/12 fl oz/1⅓ cups water
250 ml/8 fl oz/1 cup crème fraîche
A few drops of almond essence (extract)
Artificial sweetener, to taste

1 Mix the gelatine with 60 ml/4 tbsp of the water in a small
bowl. Leave to soften for 5 minutes.

2 Stand the bowl in a pan of gently simmering water and stir
until completely dissolved or heat briefly in the microwave
– but do not allow to boil.

3 Stir in the remaining cold water, then whisk in three-
quarters of the crème fraîche. Add almond essence and
sweetener to taste.

4 Pour into small glass dishes and chill until set. Top with the
remaining crème fraîche before serving.

Lacy soya crêpes with lemon

*These low-carb crêpes can be served hot or cold, and stuffed
with sweet or savoury fillings as with ordinary pancakes. They
can be shredded to use in place of pasta and freeze well.*

SERVES 4 (12 SMALL PANCAKES)
CARBOHYDRATES: 3 G PER SERVING

For the pancakes:
50 g/2 oz/½ cup full-fat soya flour
A pinch of salt
75 ml/5 tbsp fortified unsweetened soya milk
75 ml/5 tbsp water
3 large eggs
Sunflower oil for shallow-frying
To finish:
Butter, artificial sweetener and lemon juice

1 Mix the flour and salt in a bowl. Whisk in the milk, water
and eggs to form a smooth batter.

2 Heat a little oil in an omelette pan and pour off the excess.
Add enough batter to just coat the base when it is swirled
around. Cook until golden underneath, then flip over and
cook the other side. Slide out of the pan and keep warm on
a plate over a pan of hot water while you cook the
remainder in the same way.

3 Smear each pancake with butter and sprinkle with sweetener and lemon juice. Roll up and serve.

Creamy mousse with strawberries

The crushed strawberries, eggs and cream in this scrumptious dessert lift it into the gourmet class! It's not worth bothering to make for one person, but it will keep in the fridge for a few days.

SERVES 4
CARBOHYDRATES: 3 G PER SERVING

1 packet of sugar-free strawberry jelly (jello) crystals
150 ml/¼ pt/⅔ cup boiling water
175 g/6 oz strawberries, hulled and sliced
2 eggs, separated
120 ml/4 fl oz /½ cup double (heavy) cream

1 Dissolve the jelly crystals in the boiling water. Make up to 300 ml/½ pt/1¼ cups with cold water.

2 Reserve four strawberry slices. Purée the remainder in a blender or food processor with the egg yolks and the jelly.

3 Chill the mixture until it has the consistency of egg white, then whisk the egg whites until stiff and the cream until peaking.

4 Fold the cream, then the egg whites into the strawberry mixture and turn into a glass dish. Chill until set and decorate with the strawberry slices before serving.

Whisky lemon syllabub

Creamy and sharp yet sweet, with a little shot of whisky for added kick, this dessert is a wonderful twist on an old favourite. The sweet-sour combination is perfect to round off a rich meal.

SERVES 4

CARBOHYDRATES: 4 G PER SERVING

Finely grated rind and juice of 1 lemon
30 ml/2 tbsp artificial sweetener
30 ml/2 tbsp whisky
250 ml/8 fl oz/1 cup single (light) cream
250 ml/8 fl oz/1 cup crème fraîche

1 Mix the lemon rind and juice with the sweetener and whisky until the sweetener has dissolved.

2 Add the cream and crème fraîche and whisk until softly peaking.

3 Spoon into four wine goblets and chill for at least 2 hours.

Strawberry and greek yoghurt sesame brûlée

A brûlée is normally made with burnt sugar, but here I use toasted sesame seeds for a golden, crisp top over plump, juicy strawberries under sweetened cream and strained yoghurt.

SERVES 4
CARBOHYDRATES: 5 G PER SERVING

225 g/8 oz strawberries, hulled and sliced
100 ml/3½ fl oz/scant ½ cup plain strained Greek-style cow's milk yoghurt
150 ml/¼ pt/⅔ cup double (heavy) cream
2.5 ml/½ tsp vanilla essence (extract)
30 ml/2 tbsp artificial sweetener
60 ml/4 tbsp sesame seeds

1 Put the strawberries in the base of four ramekin dishes (custard cups).

2 Whip the yoghurt with the cream, vanilla and sweetener until thick. Spoon the mixture over the strawberries and chill until ready to serve.

3 Preheat the grill (broiler). Sprinkle the tops liberally with the sesame seeds and grill (broil) until golden. Serve straight away.

Hazelnut cream with raspberry coulis

A delicious nutty set cream with a smooth raspberry sauce, this is ideal for entertaining. If you are eating alone, make half the quantity and enjoy it the next day as well.

SERVES 4

CARBOHYDRATES: 5 G PER SERVING

25 g/1 oz/¼ cup hazelnuts (filberts)

2 eggs

450 ml/¾ pt/2 cups double (heavy) cream

30 ml/2 tbsp artificial sweetener

A few drops of vanilla essence (extract)

A little oil for greasing

For the coulis:

175 g/6 oz fresh raspberries

A pinch of artificial sweetener

A squeeze of lemon juice

4 small sprigs of fresh mint, to decorate

1 Grind the hazelnuts in a blender or food processor until finely ground.

2 Whisk the eggs, then whisk in the cream and sweeten with the artificial sweetener and vanilla. Stir in the nuts.

3 Lightly oil four ramekin dishes (custard cups) and pour in the cream mixture. Place in a frying pan (skillet) with enough boiling water to come half-way up the sides of the dishes. Cover the pan with a lid or foil and simmer over a very low heat for about 30 minutes until set. Do not heat quickly or the mixture will curdle.

4 Remove the dishes from the pan, leave to cool, then chill in the fridge.

5 Meanwhile, to make the coulis, purée the raspberries in a blender or food processor and sweeten to taste. Sharpen with a squeeze of lemon juice. Pass the mixture through a fine sieve (strainer) into a bowl. Chill.

6 When ready to serve, loosen the edges and turn the creams out on to small plates. Trickle the raspberry coulis around and decorate each with a small sprig of mint.

Mandarin orange cheese sherbet

A frozen dessert of cottage cheese blended with freshly squeezed mandarin orange juice and a hint of spices to make a delicious low-carbohydrate dessert fit for any occasion.

SERVES 4

CARBOHYDRATES: 5 G PER SERVING

2 mandarin oranges
225 g/8 oz/1 cup cottage cheese
30 ml/2 tbsp artificial sweetener
A pinch of ground mixed (apple-pie) spice
1 egg white

1 Grate the zest of one of the mandarins, thinly pare the zest from the other and squeeze the juice from both. Cut the pared zest into thin strips and boil in water for 2 minutes. Drain, rinse with cold water and drain again.

2 Blend the grated zest, juice, cheese, sweetener and spice until smooth. Alternatively, pass the cheese through a fine sieve (strainer) and beat in the other ingredients.

3 Turn the mixture into a shallow freezer-proof container, cover with foil and freeze for 2 hours.

4 Remove the mixture from the freezer and whisk with a fork to break up the ice crystals. Whisk the egg white until stiff and fold into the mixture with a metal spoon. Re-cover and return to the freezer. Freeze for a further 1½ hours, then whisk with a fork again to break up the ice crystals.

5 Return the cheese sherbet to the freezer and freeze until firm.

6 When ready to serve, scoop the sherbet into wine goblets and sprinkle with the thinly pared mandarin zest.

Low-carb Italian tiramisu

*Low-carb bread works just as well as sponge cake in this dessert.
The name means 'pick-me-up' and it will do just that, with its
coffee-and-brandy base beneath Mascarpone and cream.*

SERVES 4
CARBOHYDRATES: 5 G PER SERVING

4 slices of Low-carbohydrate Soya Bread (see page 102)
15 ml/1 tbsp instant coffee granules
120 ml/4 fl oz/½ cup hot water
30 ml/2 tbsp artificial sweetener
45 ml/3 tbsp brandy
225 g/8 oz/1 cup Mascarpone cheese
150 ml/¼ pt/⅔ cup double (heavy) cream, whipped
A little ground cinnamon

1   Put the bread slices in the base of four individual dishes.
    Mix the coffee in the water until dissolved and sweeten
    with 20 ml/4 tsp of the artificial sweetener. Stir in half the
    brandy. Spoon over the bread to cover completely and mash
    with a fork to soak in thoroughly.

2   Beat the Mascarpone with the remaining brandy and the
    remaining sweetener. Spread over the coffee mixture.

3   Cover with whipped cream and decorate the tops with a
    dusting of cinnamon. Chill until ready to serve.

Index

Index

Index